# ILTS Physical Education 144

## Illinois Licensure Testing System

## By: Preparing Teachers In America™

This page is intentionally left blank.

This page is intentionally left blank.

## Free Online Email Tutoring Services

All preparation guides purchased directly from Preparing Teachers In America includes a free three month email tutoring subscription. Any resale of preparation guides does not qualify for a free email tutoring subscription.

### What is Email Tutoring?

Email Tutoring allows buyers to send questions to tutors via email. Buyers can send any questions regarding the exam processes, strategies, content questions, or practice questions.

Preparing Teachers In America reserves the right not to answer questions with or without reason(s).

### How to use Email Tutoring?

Buyers need to send an email to onlinepreparationservices@gmail.com requesting email tutoring services. Buyers may be required to confirm the email address used to purchase the preparation guide or additional information prior to using email tutoring. Once email tutoring subscription is confirmed, buyers will be provided an email address to send questions to. The three month period will start the day the subscription is confirmed.

Any misuse of email tutoring services will result in termination of service. Preparing Teachers In America reserves the right to terminate email tutoring subscription at anytime with or without notice.

### Comments and Suggestions

All comments and suggestions for improvements for the study guide and email tutoring services need to be sent to onlinepreparationservices@gmail.com.

This page is intentionally left blank.

# Table of Content

This page is intentionally left blank.

## About the Exam and Study Guide

**What is the ILTS Physical Education Exam?**

The ILTS Physical Education is an exam to measure potential teachers' competencies in physical education knowledge from elementary through high schools. The test measures if individuals have the knowledge necessary to start teaching physical education. The exam is based largely on teacher preparation standards, and the following are content areas covered by the physical education exam:

- Growth and Motor Development
- Movement Activities
- Lifelong Physical Fitness
- The Physical Education Program

The exam is timed at 225 minutes and consists of 125 questions. The 125 selected-response questions are based on knowledge obtained in a bachelor's degree program. The exam contains some questions that may not count toward the score.

**What topics are covered on the exam?**

The following are some topics covered on the exam:

- characteristics of human growth and development
- movement and physical fitness
- motor development and motor learning
- principles of biomechanics
- safety practices for physical activities
- health-related physical fitness
- developing and maintaining physical activity
- plan, implement, and evaluate physical education in instructional activities
- legal, professional, and safety guidelines
- anatomy and physiology
- exercise physiology
- classroom management practices
- appropriate communication techniques

**What is included in this study guide book?**

This guide includes one full length practice exam for the ILTS Physical Education along with detail explanations. The recommendation is to take the exam under exam conditions of 225 minutes and a quiet environment.

This page is intentionally left blank.

# Practice Test 1

This page is intentionally left blank.

# Exam Answer Sheet

Below is an optional answer sheet to use to document answers.

| Question Number | Selected Answer | Question Number | Selected Answer | Question Number | Selected Answer | Question Number | Selected Answer | Question Number | Selected Answer |
|---|---|---|---|---|---|---|---|---|---|
| 1 | | 31 | | 61 | | 91 | | 121 | |
| 2 | | 32 | | 62 | | 92 | | 122 | |
| 3 | | 33 | | 63 | | 93 | | 123 | |
| 4 | | 34 | | 64 | | 94 | | 124 | |
| 5 | | 35 | | 65 | | 95 | | 125 | |
| 6 | | 36 | | 66 | | 96 | | | |
| 7 | | 37 | | 67 | | 97 | | | |
| 8 | | 38 | | 68 | | 98 | | | |
| 9 | | 39 | | 69 | | 99 | | | |
| 10 | | 40 | | 70 | | 100 | | | |
| 11 | | 41 | | 71 | | 101 | | | |
| 12 | | 42 | | 72 | | 102 | | | |
| 13 | | 43 | | 73 | | 103 | | | |
| 14 | | 44 | | 74 | | 104 | | | |
| 15 | | 45 | | 75 | | 105 | | | |
| 16 | | 46 | | 76 | | 106 | | | |
| 17 | | 47 | | 77 | | 107 | | | |
| 18 | | 48 | | 78 | | 108 | | | |
| 19 | | 49 | | 79 | | 109 | | | |
| 20 | | 50 | | 80 | | 110 | | | |
| 21 | | 51 | | 81 | | 111 | | | |
| 22 | | 52 | | 82 | | 112 | | | |
| 23 | | 53 | | 83 | | 113 | | | |
| 24 | | 54 | | 84 | | 114 | | | |
| 25 | | 55 | | 85 | | 115 | | | |
| 26 | | 56 | | 86 | | 116 | | | |
| 27 | | 57 | | 87 | | 117 | | | |
| 28 | | 58 | | 88 | | 118 | | | |
| 29 | | 59 | | 89 | | 119 | | | |
| 30 | | 60 | | 90 | | 120 | | | |

This page is intentionally left blank.

# Physical Education Exam Questions

## QUESTION 1

A physical education teacher is exhausted in class. Which of the following is the best approach for the teacher to undertake?

- A. have more influence on the curriculum selection
- B. limit the amount of physical activities
- C. engage in more wellness activities
- D. get an assistant to help out during activities

**Answer:**

## QUESTION 2

A physical education teacher plans to use sit-and-reach test in a coming lesson to assess an individual's physical fitness level. This test is best used for evaluating:

- A. endurance
- B. flexibility
- C. strength
- D. motor skills

**Answer:**

## QUESTION 3

In terms of reaction time, how is it best to absorb a force?

- A. decrease time and distance
- B. increase time and distance
- C. decrease distance
- D. increase distance

**Answer:**

**QUESTION 4**

Jake is a first grade student, and he is avoiding ladders and grab bars. In addition, while his friends play in the jungle gym, Jake is avoiding the jungle gym. The teacher observes the student is unable to determine what to hold onto or pull up onto to climb the structure. The student has difficulty in:

    A. understanding the purpose of the different types of structures
    B. maintaining eye coordination
    C. discerning features that will help him climb due to a visual deficit
    D. interacting with the students during physical activities

**Answer:**

**QUESTION 5**

In developing a motor task analysis of a particular skill, the first step should be to:

    A. understand the purpose
    B. break the skill into continuous steps
    C. know the grade level
    D. define the skill

**Answer:**

**QUESTION 6**

    I.     Ensure the ball is close to the feet
    II.    Remain in a slightly crouched position
    III.   Use only the dominant foot for better control

Which of the above should a player attempt to do when dribbling a soccer ball in a restricted space?

    A. I only
    B. II only
    C. I and II
    D. I and III

**Answer:**

## QUESTION 7

_____ is a locomotor skill where a foot finishes two tasks before the weight is passed on to the other foot.

    A. Running

    B. Jogging

    C. Skipping

    D. Walking

**Answer:**

## QUESTION 8

Martin is a swimmer, and during practice, he maintains a straight body with the legs near the surface. This results in:

    A. reducing the drag from the water on Martin

    B. decreasing Martin's speed during swimming

    C. increasing Martin's buoyancy

    D. increasing the potential energy on Martin

**Answer:**

## QUESTION 9

Which of the following is true about the principle of gravity?

    A. a wider base of support is easier than a narrow base of support

    B. during a static balance the line of gravity should go through the base of the support

    C. leaning over the line of gravity should be countered with extension of the body part in opposite direction

    D. during a dynamic activity the line of gravity should go through the base of the support

**Answer:**

**QUESTION 10**

    I.     located in the front, top half of the arm

    II.    function is to flex the elbow

    III.   used when carrying things

The above describes which part of the muscular system:

    A.  abdominals

    B.  biceps

    C.  triceps

    D.  pectorals

**Answer:**

**QUESTION 11**

What muscle extends the elbow in an overhead throw?

    A.  biceps

    B.  triceps

    C.  pectorals

    D.  deltoids

**Answer:**

**QUESTION 12**

Which of the following activities is not appropriate for K-12 school physical education programs?

    A.  volleyball

    B.  dodgeball

    C.  hockey

    D.  climbing

**Answer:**

## QUESTION 13

Which of the following requires that students with disabilities receive specially designed physical education services, if necessary?

    A.  IDEA 2004

    B.  IDEA 2010

    C.  IEP

    D.  NASPE

**Answer:**

## QUESTION 14

Before children learn how to properly skip, what locomotor skill should they learn?

    A.  hopping

    B.  galloping

    C.  sliding

    D.  kicking

**Answer:**

## QUESTION 15

Which of the following is best first to learn when swimming?

    A.  flutter kick

    B.  whip kick

    C.  breaststroke

    D.  gliding

**Answer:**

## QUESTION 16

In theory, when running, what is the proper direction the legs should be moving?

    A.  back and forth

    B.  up and down

    C.  in a cycle

    D.  sideways

**Answer:**

## QUESTION 17

When individuals are constantly involved in resistance weight training, they are likely to benefit the body by:

    A.  decreasing chances of heart disease

    B.  increasing bone density

    C.  increasing blood flow

    D.  decreasing joint dismemberment

**Answer:**

## QUESTION 18

What does the sergeant jump test measure?

    A.  agility

    B.  strength

    C.  height

    D.  speed

**Answer:**

## QUESTION 19

    I.      cyclist's knees

    II.     swimmer's arms

    III.    runner's legs

Of the above, which of the following displays the concept of angular motion?

    A.  I only
    B.  I and II
    C.  I and III
    D.  I, II and III

**Answer:**

## QUESTION 20

Which of the following is most critical for the sport of golf?

    A.  agility
    B.  coordination
    C.  balance
    D.  speed

**Answer:**

## QUESTION 21

    I.      motor learning

    II.     kinesiology

    III.    biomechanics

Of the above disciplines, which are the foundation(s) for physical education?

    A.  I only
    B.  I and II
    C.  II and III
    D.  I, II, and III

**Answer:**

**QUESTION 22**

In physical education lesson planning, there is a concern of liability. Which of the following is not a way to avoid negligence claims?

A. Following procedures and practices that are addressed in national organization guidelines.

B. Explaining new activities in detail to students prior to starting the activities.

C. Ensuring students are properly and safely executing activities.

D. Maintaining an active, ongoing process of supervision throughout activities.

**Answer:**

**QUESTION 23**

Which of the following assessments is best used to assess the fitness f students with disabilities?

A. Fitnessgram

B. ActivityGram

C. President's Challenge

D. Brockport Physical Fitness Test

**Answer:**

**QUESTION 24**

Swimming three-fourths of a mile three times a week is most likely to develop which of the following?

A. balance

B. agility

C. strength

D. aerobic fitness

**Answer:**

## QUESTION 25

Tennis player A had player B off balance and near the net, what kind of shot should player A perform?

   A. backhand drive

   B. lob

   C. drop

   D. forehand drive

**Answer:**

## QUESTION 26

Having a third grade student use one leg and one hand to static balance is most useful for:

   A. increasing strength

   B. developing agility

   C. increasing endurance

   D. developing body awareness

**Answer:**

## QUESTION 27

_____ is a sub-discipline of physical education that focuses on the effects of various physical demands, particularly exercise, on the structure and function of the body.

   A. Motor development

   B. Exercise physiology

   C. Exercise biomechanics

   D. Exercise psychology

**Answer:**

## QUESTION 28

Which of the following is a similarity in physical education, exercise science, and sport?

    A.  aerobic activity

    B.  physical activity

    C.  aerobic activity

    D.  strength activity

**Answer:**

## QUESTION 29

Which of the following is a goal of Healthy People 2010?

    A.  increase the graduation rate from junior high school

    B.  increase years of healthy life

    C.  eliminate health inconsistencies

    D.  both B and C

**Answer:**

## QUESTION 30

The back-saver sit and reach test is used to measure which of the following?

    A.  hamstring flexibility

    B.  trunk flexibility

    C.  lower back strength

    D.  upper back strength

**Answer:**

**QUESTION 31**

Which of the following groups' created around the 1840s and 1850s results in growth of physical education?

  A. YMCA
  B. NASPE
  C. YWCA
  D. SHAPE

**Answer:**

**QUESTION 32**

Which of the following most likely results in enhancing an adolescent's sense of self-worth?

  A. engaging in team activities in positive manner
  B. working toward goals
  C. implementing rules of games
  D. creating new games and sports

**Answer:**

**QUESTION 33**

When constructing a test to assess students' knowledge at the completion of a unit on physical education foundation, which of the following is most critical for the assessment?

  A. to test students at the end of the activity
  B. to test content that is aligned to the defined learning goals of the unit
  C. to take into account students with learning disabilities
  D. to understand that not all students will have the same knowledge

**Answer:**

## QUESTION 34

At the end of a unit on soccer, Mr. Locke is seeking to determine what the students have learned. Which of the following assessments is the best to implement?

A. authentic assessment
B. standards-based assessment
C. summative assessment
D. norm-referenced assessment

**Answer:**

## QUESTION 35

Mr. Locke, a high school teacher, is teaching a foundational lesson on throwing a football. He knows that his students have a natural understanding of the topic going into it. He is intending to understand what they know before he begins the unit. He will use their prior knowledge to create activities to help them understand the concepts involved in throwing a football. Which of the following assessments is best for Mr. Locke?

A. criterion-based assessment
B. norms-based assessment
C. formative assessment
D. authentic assessment

**Answer:**

## QUESTION 36

Which of the following types of assessments includes a variety of samples of a student's work, collected overtime, that shows the student's growth and development?

A. anecdotal records
B. portfolio
C. running record
D. grades

**Answer:**

## QUESTION 37

     I.     a portfolio
    II.    an intelligence test
   III.   an adaptive behavior scale

Of the above, which of the following is/are formal assessment(s)?

  A.  I and II
  B.  I and III
  C.  II and III
  D.  I, II, and III

**Answer:**

## QUESTION 38

A teacher is seeking to find out if students have mastered the instructional objectives at the end of a unit. What type of assessment is the best to use?

  A.  norm referenced
  B.  achievement
  C.  diagnostic
  D.  placement

**Answer:**

## QUESTION 39

Which of the following assessments is used to evaluate student learning at the conclusion of an instructional period (ex. at the end of a unit)?

  A.  formative assessment
  B.  interim assessment
  C.  summative assessment
  D.  placement assessment

**Answer:**

**QUESTION 40**

A middle school teacher is looking to use an informal assessment to capture overall learning. Which of the following is the best option?

A. authentic assessment
B. graded homework
C. exit card
D. performance assessment

**Answer:**

**QUESTION 41**

Ongoing observation in authentic contexts with which the student is customary to and has had opportunities to practice is most appropriately used when assessing student's progress in

_____.

A. physical education content knowledge
B. motor performance
C. team competition
D. playing soccer

**Answer:**

**QUESTION 42**

What reflex in children up to 5 years old can affect the gross motor skill of catching a ball?

A. ball handling
B. throwing
C. kicking
D. bending

**Answer:**

**QUESTION 43**

A teacher walks in the room and a child is lying on the ground unconscious. What is the first action the teacher should take?

    A.  remove any surrounding objects that might cause more harm to the student

    B.  perform CPR

    C.  leave the scene and call 911

    D.  call the school nurse

**Answer:**

**QUESTION 44**

Jenny's dad promised that he is going to attend the basketball game. However, he ended up having to go work. With the dad not showing up for the game, Jenny's _____ is most impacted.

    A.  self-discipline

    B.  self-esteem

    C.  social interaction

    D.  self-image

**Answer:**

**QUESTION 45**

What is the best warm-up for the front crawl in swimming?

    A.  dragging fingers along the top of the water and raising the elbow higher

    B.  running in shallow water

    C.  stretching and performing a warm up routine

    D.  practice keeping the body positioned flatly to be streamlined in the water

**Answer:**

**QUESTION 46**

In track and field events, starting blocks are most commonly used in which event?

    A. long jumps
    B. distance running
    C. running
    D. sprints

**Answer:**

**QUESTION 47**

A 15-year-old student whose heart rate is 130 beats per minutes would be considered to be:

    A. at ventilatory threshold
    B. performing submaximal exercise
    C. performing maximal exercise
    D. hyperventilating

**Answer:**

**QUESTION 48**

Jimmy is looking to lose weight and build endurance, so the key target zone is 60% of his maximum heart rate. Jimmy is 30 years old. What is his maximum heart rate for the key target zone?

    A. 100
    B. 114
    C. 130
    D. 190

**Answer:**

**QUESTION 49**

Medical attention is required when blood pressure becomes higher than:

A. 180/110

B. 145/90

C. 120/80

D. 150/100

**Answer:**

**QUESTION 50**

The moment of inertia is greatest when more mass is at a _____ distance from the axis of rotation.

A. lesser

B. greater

C. equal

D. center

**Answer:**

**QUESTION 51**

Which of the following causes possible excessive vomiting, tremors, sweating and anxiety?

A. stimulants

B. depressants

C. painkillers

D. anabolic steroids

**Answer:**

## QUESTION 52

Which of the following is the best reflective assessment for a group of elementary education students learning about basics of soccer?

    A. Ask students to think about what they learned, and then write out their reflection in a sentence with "I learned ...."

    B. Ask students to complete a worksheet that has questions related to the content presented to them.

    C. Ask students to write down key concepts during reflective assessment.

    D. Ask students to draw what they remember about the content presented to them.

**Answer:**

## QUESTION 53

Which of the following societies stands for health and physical education?

    A. SHAPE

    B. NATA

    C. NCCEA

    D. NECA

**Answer:**

## QUESTION 54

Emily stretched her ligaments in her calf, which is considered a

    A. strain

    B. sprain

    C. heat cramp

    D. stress

**Answer:**

**QUESTION 55**

Which of the following has the most caffeine?

    A.  8 oz coffee

    B.  8 oz tea

    C.  12 oz soda

    D.  a chocolate bar

**Answer:**

**QUESTION 56**

To improve his kicking skills for soccer, Drew's trainer recommended that he train with a leg-extension exercise, along with gradually increasing its weight to increase his strength. The leg extension exercise works the _____ muscle.

    A.  trapezius

    B.  hamstring

    C.  gluteus maximus

    D.  quadriceps

**Answer:**

**QUESTION 57**

In football, a player should extend his or her kicking leg when contacting a football during a punt. Which of the following is the best reason for undertaking such a move?

    A.  to allow for greater distance and time to apply the force to the football with the kicking foot

    B.  to increase the radius from the axis of rotation, the hip joint, which results in the kicking foot moving faster than any other part of the leg on contact

    C.  to reduce the force of interaction between the kicking foot and the ball

    D.  to lessen the reaction of the force being exerted and decrease the flexing of the leg

**Answer:**

**QUESTION 58**

A physical education instructor in her swimming class is telling her fifth grade students to point toes like a diver, kick heels, and roll chin to shoulder. The teacher's intention is most likely to help the students swim more effectively by:

A. encouraging teamwork
B. placing less stress on the knees
C. reducing the effects of drag by the water movement
D. increasing energy during activity

**Answer:**

**QUESTION 59**

During physical education class, a group of third-graders see that some students are better at balancing, some are better at tumbling, and some are better at jumping. As a result, the teacher informs the students that everyone is good at different things and everybody can improve with practice. The teacher's response to her class shows that the teacher's awareness of the role of physical education is:

A. establishing competition as students see different level of skills
B. teaching awareness and respect for diverse talents and abilities
C. ensuring all students get a opportunities to improve
D. promoting students' integration via of nonlocomotor and locomotor skills.

**Answer:**

**QUESTION 60**

Which of the following best describes activities that will increase the cardio-respiratory capacity and includes dynamic stretches?

A. low-intensity aerobic activities
B. moderate-intensity aerobic activities
C. high-intensity aerobic activities
D. none of the above

**Answer:**

**QUESTION 61**

A physical education teacher is looking to incorporate biomechanical concepts in her classroom as part of cross curriculum. The teacher wants to ensure students understand the application of static and dynamic balance skills. To ensure state standards of cross curriculum are satisfied, which of the following biomechanical concepts can be best implemented in her lesson?

    A. kinetic energy
    B. potential energy
    C. center of gravity
    D. centripetal force

**Answer:**

**QUESTION 62**

As individuals develop, the hypothalamus signals the pituitary gland to release growth hormone and causes the production of thyroxine, resulting in gains in body size and skeletal growth. The increase in this substance is a result primarily o f what two body systems interaction?

    A. skeletal system and muscular system
    B. skeletal system and nervous system
    C. respiratory system and skeletal system
    D. nervous system and endocrine system

**Answer:**

**QUESTION 63**

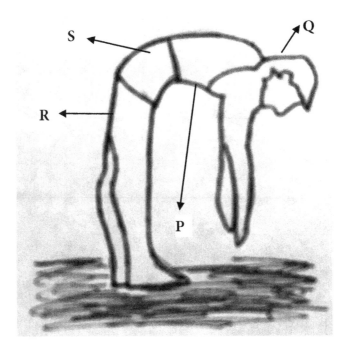

In the above image, which of the following locates the center of gravity?

   A. Q
   B. P
   C. R
   D. S

**Answer:**

**QUESTION 64**

Pushing, bouncing, circling, and twisting are best described as?

   A. locomotors skills

   B. specialized skills

   C. nonlocomotor skills

   D. manipulative skills

**Answer:**

**QUESTION 65**

Standard 2 of the National Standards for Physical Education states the following: "Demonstrates understanding of movement concepts, principles, strategies, and tactics as they apply to the learning and performance of physical activities." Of the following which does not display Standard 2?

A. During soccer practice, the teacher tells the students to place their nonkicking feet alongside the ball to create velocity in their kicking feet.

B. The teacher tells students to bring the ball back behind their heads with their elbows bent to increase the distance throw.

C. The teacher tells the students to use their heads for ball movement.

D. The teacher tells students to flex their tuck and tend their arms with strength and directly overhead on the release.

**Answer:**

**QUESTION 66**

|     | Word | Definition |
| --- | --- | --- |
| I | Muscular Strength | the ability of the muscle to continue to perform without fatigue. |
| II | Muscular Endurance | the maximum amount of force a muscle can produce in a single effort. |
| III | Body Composition | the ratio of lean tissue to fat tissue in the body. |
| IV | Cardio Respiratory Endurance | the ability of the circulatory and respiratory systems to supply oxygen during sustained physical activity. |

In the above table, which of the following is incorrectly defined?

    A. I only

    B. II only

    C. I and II

    D. II, III, and IV

**Answer:**

**QUESTION 67**

Which of the following correctly defines balance, time, force, and flow?

A.

Balance: Understand the nature of static and dynamic balance and the role of balance in movement.
Time: Differentiate among speeds and to increase or decrease the speed of movement.
Force: To be able to create and modify one's force to meet the demands of the task
Flow: To combine movements smoothly and to perform movements within a restricted time or space

B.

Balance: Differentiate among speeds and to increase or decrease the speed of movement.
Time: Understand the nature of static and dynamic balance and the role of balance in movement.
Force: To be able to create and modify one's force to meet the demands of the task
Flow: To combine movements smoothly and to perform movements within a restricted time or space

C.

Balance: Differentiate among speeds and to increase or decrease the speed of movement.
Time: Understand the nature of static and dynamic balance and the role of balance in movement.
Force: To combine movements smoothly and to perform movements within a restricted time or space .
Flow: To be able to create and modify one's force to meet the demands of the task

D.

Balance: To combine movements smoothly and to perform movements within a restricted time or space.
Time: Differentiate among speeds and to increase or decrease the speed of movement.
Force: To be able to create and modify one's force to meet the demands of the task
Flow: Understand the nature of static and dynamic balance and the role of balance in movement.

**Answer:**

## QUESTION 68

Which of the following is not a non-locomotor movement?

    A. lifting

    B. rotating

    C. jogging

    D. flexing

**Answer:**

## QUESTION 69

A physical education teacher instructs a student to push his elbow toward his chest and hold the stretch for 20 seconds. Which of the following muscles are being targeted here?

    A. brachialis

    B. deltoid

    C. latissimus

    D. rotator cuff

**Answer:**

## QUESTION 70

Aerial tumbling moves require safety precautions. Which of the following safety precautions is most critical in practicing flips and somersaults?

    A. wearing proper equipment

    B. having qualified spotters

    C. using triple-thickness mats

    D. practice slowly prior to going full force

**Answer:**

## QUESTION 71

A physical education teacher has constructed an activity where students will walk in and around large hoop placed on the floor. This activity is most useful in developing which of the following fundamental skills?

    A.  spatial awareness
    B.  rhythmic movement
    C.  static balance
    D.  locomotive skills

**Answer:**

## QUESTION 72

Matt sees a flyer for a weight-loss pill that states the pill can cause someone to lose 15 pounds in only 7 days. The flyer says that the pill is all natural and healthy. Which of the following is the best action for Curtis to take to make sure that this product is safe to use?

    A.  compare the advertisements of different weight losing pills
    B.  complete an online research on the pill and company offering the pill
    C.  start a diet while taking the weight-loss pill
    D.  ask a friend about the product

**Answer:**

## QUESTION 73

A tenth grade student desires to improve cardio-respiratory endurance along with reducing body fat. The student has decided to implement the following plan:

Frequency of Workout: 7 days a week

Intensity of Workout: Moderate

Work out Details:

I.    Warm-up (20 minutes): Jogging in place with dynamic stretching
II.   Cycling for 40 minutes
III.  Cool down (15 minutes): Walking with flexibility exercises

Which of the following modification will best help to ensure the student's goal is achieved?

A.  increase the time of teaching  activity by 10 minutes
B.  add several components related to resistance or weight training
C.  implement robust exercise activities
D.  implement the plan outlined in the mornings and nights

**Answer:**

## QUESTION 74

I.    to respond readily to instructions
II.   to follow rules, codes, and safety practices
III.  to work with other students to ensure learning
IV.   to warm up and recover from exercise

Which of the following are ways to teach students on ensuring safe practices are being implemented in physical education classrooms?

A.  I and II
B.  II and III
C.  I, II, and IV
D.  II, III, and IV

**Answer:**

**QUESTION 75**

As a physical education teacher, promoting health education is a central responsibility. A physical education teacher is communicating the negatives of smoking while the teacher has the habit of smoking. Another physical education teacher is prompting healthy eating, while noticeably overweight. These physical education teachers are implementing which type of communication?

    A. verbal communication

    B. non-verbal communication

    C. contradicting messages

    D. unintentional communication

**Answer:**

**QUESTION 76**

Engaging the entire family in a healthy eating plan is most likely the best approach in which of the following?

    A. Supporting elementary students to eating healthy.

    B. Supporting an adolescent in losing weight.

    C. Teaching kids on importance of eating healthy.

    D. Supporting state curriculum of teaching healthy eating at home.

**Answer:**

**QUESTION 77**

Which of the following activities is considered a true net/wall game?

    A. badminton

    B. hiking

    C. lacrosse

    D. soccer

**Answer:**

**QUESTION 78**

In school classes, folk dances for grade K-12 are best when emphasizing:

    A. polka steps
    B. tinkling steps
    C. locomotor skills
    D. manipulative skills

**Answer:**

**QUESTION 79**

Which of the following is the best way to learn about the best practices to start teaching physical education during first year of instructing?

    A. Give students a survey on the teaching methods being implemented in the classroom, so teachers obtain feedback on improvement.
    B. Observe lessons taught by an experienced physical education teachers and note the types of activity in which there are involved, their sequence, and the time spent on the lesson.
    C. Undergo yearly professional training on teaching methods for physical education curriculum.
    D. Set monthly meetings with principals or mentors on obtaining feedback on teaching.

**Answer:**

## QUESTION 80

I.   balance
II.  speed
III. strength
IV.  coordination

Agility is the ability to change the direction of the body in an efficient and effective manner. To achieve this, which of the following is required?

A. I and II
B. I, II, and III
C. I, III, and IV
D. I, II, III, and IV

**Answer:**

## QUESTION 81

Once a physical education instructor has taught a lesson or part of a lesson, and before the thinking of planning the next lesson, instructor needs to evaluate the effectiveness of the current lesson. Which of the following reasons is not correct for undertaking this approach?

A. Essential part of capturing student learning along with instructor learning and ensure progress of student.
B. To document student progress to be able to make comparison analysis of student progress.
C. Ensure objectives of the lesson were achieved, but also whether the objectives were, in fact, realistic and appropriate.
D. To support instructor in developing future lesson.

**Answer:**

## QUESTION 82

A physical education teacher has an instructional unit on basketball that addresses basic dribbling, passing, and shooting skills along with techniques such as drills, partner work, and modified games. Half the course is often used with the basket typically lowered below the regulation height. This instructional unit best describes which grade level?

A. second grade
B. fourth grade
C. eight grade
D. night grade

**Answer:**

**QUESTION 83**

The following diagram shows a process an instructor uses to monitor movements in physical activities.

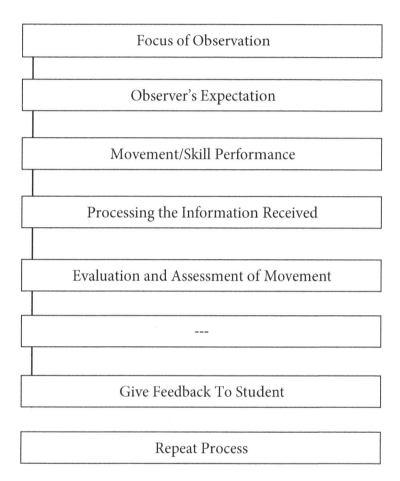

Which of the following is best to place in the blank box above?

- A.  Document assessment in grade book
- B.  Compare results with other classroom students
- C.  Evaluate effectiveness of assessment
- D.  Priorities and plan feedback

**Answer:**

## QUESTION 84

Various forms of assessments are used in the physical education classroom. Assessments that allow ongoing feedback to progress toward skill learning goals are called:

- A. summative assessments
- B. formative assessments
- C. formal assessments
- D. informal assessments

**Answer:**

## QUESTION 85

Which of the following is best describes a formal assessment?

- A. performing a standardized skill test from a sport (such as a kicking a soccer ball to make a goal)
- B. observing players passing the ball in a game and remembering the level of passing performance
- C. using a list to assess performance in a game
- D. using a scale to assess performance in a game

**Answer:**

## QUESTION 86

During a creative arts seminar, several juggling stations are set up that are devoted to the physical education department. Different objects such as scarves, balls, beanbags and small plastic hoops are available. Students may move to different stations at will and may juggle with multiple objects. Which of the following is primary advantage of this type of setup?

- A. it displays to everyone that physical education involves multiple activities and cross curriculum
- B. it minimizes the possibility that students will get bored
- C. it gives students choices in deciding entry levels into the activity
- D. it gives students the opportunity to think which activity is hardest to complete

**Answer:**

## QUESTION 87

The Fitnessgram physical fitness assessment program places its highest priority on:

- A. comparing student scores within the same age group
- B. helping school children to be active
- C. developing health-related behaviors to be attained by students
- D. high fitness performance

**Answer:**

## QUESTION 88

The goal of a secondary physical education program is to prompt the value of teamwork and teach cooperative skills. Which of the following activities will support the goal of the secondary physical education school program?

- A. In a soccer game, have students who are rotated out of the game to support teammates with positive comments.
- B. In a soccer game, have students focus on passing while simultaneously playing their own positions in practice games.
- C. Have students select teammates at the start of the school year and have them work with the same teammates throughout the school year.
- D. Pair students who lag in physical activities to those who are progressing in a positive direction toward the goal.

**Answer:**

## QUESTION 89

Which of the following are responsible for controlling muscular movement of the head, neck, body and limbs and transmitting the nerve impulses to the central nervous system after receiving a signal respectively?

- A. sympathetic nerve; parasympathetic nerve
- B. central nerve; autonomic nerve
- C. parasympathetic nerve; central nerve
- D. motor nerve; sensory nerve

**Answer:**

## QUESTION 90

| Week | Sets | Repetitions | Load (kg) | Rest (s) |
|------|------|-------------|-----------|----------|
| 1 | 2 | 10 | 60 | 40 |
| 2 | 3 | 12 | 65 | 35 |
| 3 | 4 | 14 | 70 | 30 |

Which of the following training principle is best illustrated in the above program?

    A. specificity
    B. reversibility
    C. variance
    D. overload

**Answer:**

## QUESTION 91

    I.    To maintain aerobic fitness.
    II.   To maintain muscular strength.
   III.  To ease the psychological stress of the sprinter.

Which of the following are the reasons why a sprinter frequently uses ball games in the training program during off-season?

    A. I and II
    B. I and III
    C. II and III
    D. I, II, and III

**Answer:**

## QUESTION 92

The ratio of one's muscle, bone and body fat to one's body weight would be an example of his/her

- A. flexibility
- B. muscular endurance
- C. body composition
- D. muscular strength

**Answer:**

## QUESTION 93

A concentric contraction causes muscles to shorten, thereby generating which of the following?

- A. sounds
- B. bonds
- C. forces
- D. distance

**Answer:**

## QUESTION 94

Which of the following hormones is produced more during the sleep cycle?

- A. melatonin
- B. somatostatin
- C. thyrotropin
- D. adrenaline

**Answer:**

## QUESTION 95

    I.       Shortened attention span

    II.     Decreased overall cognitive performance

    III.    Ineffective at self control

    IV.    Unable to achieve academically

Iron is a dietary mineral that is critical for various bodily functions, including the transport of oxygen in the blood. Which of the following is/are signs of iron deficiency in students?

    A.  I, II and III

    B.  I, II, and IV

    C.  I, III, and IV

    D.  II, III, and IV

**Answer:**

## QUESTION 96

Nutrition, weight control, understanding muscular movement, and controlling postures are components of which of the following?

    A.  physical education

    B.  wellness

    C.  healthy eating

    D.  health education

**Answer:**

## QUESTION 97

Fitness plans that call for slowly adding weights or increasing resistance with each workout are called _____.

    A.  slow resistance

    B.  overload resistance

    C.  steady resistance

    D.  progressive resistance

**Answer:**

## QUESTION 98

What does sodium help regulate?

- A.  muscles
- B.  heart
- C.  lungs
- D.  eyes

**Answer:**

## QUESTION 99

Body converts calories from food to energy. This is called _____.

- A.  metabolism
- B.  nutrition
- C.  energy conservation
- D.  all the above

**Answer:**

## QUESTION 100

Piaget suggests which of the following is/are the basis for all intellectual functioning for approximately the first 2 years of life?

- A.  sensory experiences
- B.  motor experiences
- C.  sensory and motor experiences
- D.  motor and cognitive development

**Answer:**

## QUESTION 101

Prior to the start of school, a physical education teacher sends a letter home informing parents of upcoming lessons on the topic of sexuality. In the letter sent, the learning goals and objectives of the lesson are described.  Regulations in states give parents or guardians the right to:

A. inform the school not to instruct the lesson to the child

B. attend the lesson to ensure the lesson is aligned with the letter provided

C. review the material prior to the lesson to decide if any information needs to be omitted

D. request to defer the lesson to a future school year

**Answer:**

## QUESTION 102

When adapting activities for physical education, classmates can use the buddy system to do which of the following to help students with hearing impairments?

A. start

B. stop

C. relay information

D. all of these

**Answer:**

## QUESTION 103

Cerebral palsy and spina bifida/hydrocephalus are neurological disorders. What factor is the most critical to understand the effect on children's motor learning?

A. see if family members have the same learning disorder

B. see if the student has cognitive and physical challenges to learning

C. see if the student has impairment issues

D. see if the student is having difficulty completing assignments.

**Answer:**

## QUESTION 104

A critical aspect of teaching physical education is having understanding of the influential factors. Of the following, which of the following is incorrect?

  A. Family situation and economic circumstances have impact on student learning.
  B. Different cultural groups may value different traditions, impacting the learning of motor skills.
  C. Environmental factor is sole impact on difference in performance of students.
  D. Various factors contribution to how students learn motor skills.

**Answer:**

## QUESTION 105

Which of the following explains how the distance and accuracy is increased, when throwing a Frisbee® by snapping the wrist sharply at the end of the throw?

  A. As the disk is thrown, additional kinetic energy is imparted which results in a farther throw.
  B. As the disk is thrown, it acts as a gyroscope and the stability is increased during the travel.
  C. As the disk is thrown, the sharp wrist movement causes conversion from static to dynamic movement.
  D. As the disk is thrown, there is a greater coefficient of friction, which reduces the drag between the disk and the air.

**Answer:**

## QUESTION 106

Which of the following displays appropriate application of the physiological principle of specificity, when planning physical education activities?

- A. Having students work in groups of four each week with different members each week.
- B. Having students complete activities that target muscle groups or energy systems that will support them in other class work.
- C. Allowing students to select class activities that interest them and rotating with teacher selected activities.
- D. Ensuring that lessons implemented in the classroom are tailored to the appropriate developmental and age level of the student

**Answer:**

**QUESTION 107**

    I.        common purpose and a commitment to achieve goals

    II.      opportunity for personal growth and social interaction

    III.    career opportunities are possible with interaction

Which of the following supports the idea that improving an adolescent's sense of self-worth is accomplished by working in team activities and having a positive contribution?

    A.  I and II

    B.  I and III

    C.  II and III

    D.  I, II, and III

**Answer:**

**QUESTION 108**

In a fourth grade classroom, individuals are working in groups to develop short original dance sequences for an upcoming school activity day. The physical education teacher gives each group a set of flashcards that has the following words:

| jump – leap – slide – rocking step – turn – spin – collapse – balance – explode … |
|---|

The requirement given to the students is to include those types of movements in their dances. By undertaking this approach, the physical education teacher is mostly improving student understanding of:

    A.  how dance can express how others are feeling in the classroom and make comparisons between movement

    B.  the role of dance composition in achieving creative expression along with the choreographic elements of dance

    C.  how to work with groups in cross curriculum activities to accomplish goals

    D.  different types of dance movements within different categories and periods in history

**Answer:**

## QUESTION 109

All of the following are benefits of a coaching career EXCEPT:

A. work with skilled and motivated individuals
B. the excitement of progressing
C. demanding time commitment to prepare for games
D. intrinsic rewards of respect

**Answer:**

## QUESTION 110

A group of seventh grade students are taking a high-ropes course after school. In doing so, the course involves climbing a rope ladder to a tree platform along with walking on a cable stretched between two trees. Which of the following is the best approach to ensure that the students are safe as they undertake this activity?

A. conduct a group meeting on the activity that is going to be completed and the safety aspects that need to be taken into consideration
B. ensure that the students wear a harness connected to an effective restraining system
C. ensure that a supervisor is available onsite to monitor the activities and that emergency contact numbers are available
D. complete the activity using ropes but with only fewer feet from the ground as a test prior to undertaking the full activity

**Answer:**

## QUESTION 111

A group of high school students are planning to go rock climbing during the early part of the summer along with running a marathon during the latter part of the summer. Completing these two activities will most likely provide what benefit to the students?

A. improve teamwork skills
B. improve health
C. improve self-image
D. improve leadership skills

**Answer:**

## QUESTION 112

Of the following, where should equipment for daily lessons be placed?

- A. away from students during attendance
- B. around perimeter of the gym
- C. back of the gym
- D. in center of the gym

**Answer:**

## QUESTION 113

A teacher is going to have students complete a new physical education activity. Of the following, which situation will most likely leave the teacher open to legal liability, if a student were injured during the activity?

- A. Having students complete an activity outside of their capability.
- B. Neglecting to inform students about safety issues and precautions related to the activity.
- C. Neglecting to inform students of the plan prior to starting activity and resulting in an injury.
- D. Focusing on one student while others are playing, ultimately resulting in an injury.

**Answer:**

## QUESTION 114

A third grade physical education teacher has students practice different locomotors skills through a unique game of tag in which students become either a snake or frog. The teacher assigns each animal type a different movement pattern and a type of prey to pursue. After being captured, an animal becomes the original species as the predator until eventually all students are the same species. Of the following, which is a best way to show the primary way that this locomotors activity builds competence in the affective domain?

- A. by giving a fun, safe opportunity to practice playing a game following the rules
- B. by giving students the chance to increase knowledge in movement skills
- C. by giving students an opportunity to see how individual contribution can impact group accomplishments
- D. by giving students a non-competitive gave in a physically safe atmosphere

**Answer:**

## QUESTION 115

A first grade student is having trouble throwing a basketball into the modified net in the gym. Which of the following modifications would be most appropriate for this student?

A.  modify the net
B.  replace the ball with a smaller ball
C.  have student use a lighter ball
D.  decrease the distance of the student from the net

**Answer:**

## QUESTION 116

Smoking, poor nutrition, inactive, and excessive sleeping are examples of what form of health risk factors?

A.  physical fitness
B.  biological factors
C.  inherited factors
D.  behavioral factors

**Answer:**

## QUESTION 117

Physical education activities need to be modified for individuals with physical disabilities. In a game of bowling, what is the best way to modify the game to accommodate individuals with physical disabilities?

A.  use lighter pins to allow the movement of pins
B.  use a ramp for rolling the ball
C.  use fewer pins
D.  give additional number of rolls

**Answer:**

**QUESTION 118**

A physical education teacher teaching a golf unit observes that one of her top student is having difficulty with techniques despite continued coaching. The physical education teacher is aware of an upcoming exhibition of a golf match. The teacher encourages the student to attend the event. By providing this encouragement the teacher is most likely intending to take advantage of which of the following learning concepts?

    A. learning motor skills via experiences individuals
    B. learning via observation
    C. learning via multimedia techniques
    D. learning via external means

**Answer:**

**QUESTION 119**

Of the following applications of technology, which will be best to help a wrestler learn a new take down technique?

    A. reading about the proper technique on the Internet
    B. viewing videos of his or her own performances
    C. viewing videos of other professional wrestlers
    D. buying technology related equipment to support physical activities

**Answer:**

## QUESTION 120

Below are the spectrum styles in regards to the teaching style in physical education. Which of the following is incorrectly matched?

| Letter | Spectrum Style | Learning Intentions | Physical Education Example |
|--------|---------------|---------------------|---------------------------|
| A | Command | Physical: Motor skill sequisition | Performing a somersault on a trampoline |
| B | Practice | Physical: Motor skill development | Groups of four practice the "dig" in volleyball |
| C | Reciprocal | Social: Working with others. Cognitive observing, analysis | In twos, practice the set shot in basketball. |
| D | Self-check | Independent thinking and increase confidence | Shot putt in athletics. Success criteria on teaching card. |

**Answer:**

## QUESTION 121

Dodgeball does provide a means of practicing some important physical skills. Which of the following is not a skill obtained through dodgeball?

    A. running
    B. hiding
    C. catching
    D. throwing

**Answer:**

## QUESTION 122

The following quote is from a paper: "Even if your child's school provides daily P.E. classes, parents should still make an effort to be active role models by enjoying 60 minutes of physical activity per day…it's a fact that active parents have active children, so to ensure children reap the benefits of physical activity, such as muscle strength, cardiovascular health, and flexibility, children need to be exposed to an active lifestyle at home."

The above quote highlights the importance of:

    A.  how school and community impact the attitude of children for physical education
    B.  how setting set times and days for periodic exercise can improve health
    C.  how parents impact the motivation of children for physical education
    D.  the importance of role a model to ensure the curriculum of physical education is improving

**Answer:**

## QUESTION 123

Of the following students, who is likely to lose weight safely?

| Letter | Name | Daily Intake (calories) | Daily Expenditure (calories) |
|--------|------|-------------------------|------------------------------|
| A | Ray | 4,000 | 4,000 |
| B | Jake | 4,000 | 3,000 |
| C | Tommy | 3,000 | 3,800 |
| D | Alex | 2,000 | 5,000 |

**Answer:**

## QUESTION 124

A physical education teacher can follow which of the following in the beginning of the school year to establish the best classroom management?

A. Invite parents to the first day of class and go over the rules
B. Post rules on the front door and around the classroom and complete introductions
C. Establish rules and review them with students, create a record-keeping system, and teach students a signal to stop activity
D. Have rules posted on walls, have open gym period, and create a record keeping system

**Answer:**

## QUESTION 125

At James Intermediate School, a second grade physical education instructor is planning an activity where she will have the students walk around the school track field. Time to time the teacher will inform the students to increase their speed until it becomes hard to communicate with their partner. In undertaking this approach, the teacher is most likely trying to increase student awareness in which of the following principles?

A. intensity
B. time
C. force
D. frequency

**Answer:**

## Physical Education Correct Answer Sheet

Below is an optional answer sheet to use to document answers.

| Question Number | Right Answer | Question Number | Right Answer | Question Number | Right Answer | Question Number | Right Answer | Question Number | Right Answer |
|---|---|---|---|---|---|---|---|---|---|
| 1 | C | 31 | A | 61 | C | 91 | A | 121 | B |
| 2 | B | 32 | A | 62 | D | 92 | C | 122 | C |
| 3 | C | 33 | B | 63 | D | 93 | C | 123 | C |
| 4 | C | 34 | C | 64 | C | 94 | A | 124 | C |
| 5 | B | 35 | C | 65 | C | 95 | B | 125 | A |
| 6 | C | 36 | B | 66 | C | 96 | B | | |
| 7 | C | 37 | C | 67 | A | 97 | C | | |
| 8 | A | 38 | B | 68 | C | 98 | A | | |
| 9 | A | 39 | C | 69 | B | 99 | A | | |
| 10 | B | 40 | C | 70 | B | 100 | C | | |
| 11 | A | 41 | B | 71 | A | 101 | A | | |
| 12 | B | 42 | A | 72 | B | 102 | D | | |
| 13 | A | 43 | B | 73 | B | 103 | B | | |
| 14 | B | 44 | B | 74 | C | 104 | C | | |
| 15 | A | 45 | A | 75 | B | 105 | B | | |
| 16 | C | 46 | D | 76 | B | 106 | B | | |
| 17 | B | 47 | B | 77 | A | 107 | A | | |
| 18 | B | 48 | B | 78 | C | 108 | B | | |
| 19 | D | 49 | A | 79 | B | 109 | C | | |
| 20 | C | 50 | B | 80 | D | 110 | B | | |
| 21 | D | 51 | A | 81 | B | 111 | C | | |
| 22 | B | 52 | A | 82 | B | 112 | B | | |
| 23 | D | 53 | A | 83 | D | 113 | B | | |
| 24 | D | 54 | A | 84 | B | 114 | A | | |
| 25 | B | 55 | A | 85 | A | 115 | C | | |
| 26 | D | 56 | D | 86 | C | 116 | D | | |
| 27 | B | 57 | B | 87 | C | 117 | B | | |
| 28 | B | 58 | C | 88 | B | 118 | A | | |
| 29 | D | 59 | B | 89 | D | 119 | B | | |
| 30 | A | 60 | B | 90 | D | 120 | D | | |

NOTE: Getting approximately 80% of the questions correct increases chances of obtaining passing score on the real exam. This varies from different states and university programs.

This page is intentionally left blank.

# Physical Education Exam Questions and Answers

## QUESTION 1

A physical education teacher is exhausted in class. Which of the following is the best approach for the teacher to undertake?

- A. have more influence on the curriculum selection
- B. limit the amount of physical activities
- C. engage in more wellness activities
- D. get an assistant to help out during activities

**Answer:** C

**Explanation:** A physical education teacher will need to engage in wellness activities to avoid being exhausted in class. A physical education should not be exhausted during class. All other options can support the physical education teacher, but the options are not best in correcting the issue.

## QUESTION 2

A physical education teacher plans to use sit-and-reach test in a coming lesson to assess an individual's physical fitness level. This test is best used for evaluating:

- A. endurance
- B. flexibility
- C. strength
- D. motor skills

**Answer:** B

**Explanation:** The sit and reach test is a common measure of flexibility, and specifically measures the flexibility of the lower back and hamstring muscles.

**QUESTION 3**

In terms of reaction time, how is it best to absorb a force?

    A.  decrease time and distance

    B.  increase time and distance

    C.  decrease distance

    D.  increase distance

**Answer:** C

**Explanation:** If the distance is decreased, there will be less distance to accelerate force.

**QUESTION 4**

Jake is a first grade student, and he is avoiding ladders and grab bars. In addition, while his friends play in the jungle gym, Jake is avoiding the jungle gym. The teacher observes the student is unable to determine what to hold onto or pull up onto to climb the structure. The student has difficulty in:

    A.  understanding the purpose of the different types of structures

    B.  maintaining eye coordination

    C.  discerning features that will help him climb  due to a visual deficit

    D.  interacting with the students during physical activities

**Answer:** C

**Explanation:** Avoiding ladders and grab bars does not imply a lack of understanding in the purpose of the structure. The activities mentioned do not require eye coordination. The question indicates no issues with interacting with students. The student does not know what to hold onto or pull up onto to climb the structure, so he avoids ladders, grab bars, and jungle gym.

## QUESTION 5

In developing a motor task analysis of a particular skill, the first step should be to:

A. understand the purpose
B. break the skill into continuous steps
C. know the grade level
D. define the skill

**Answer:** B

**Explanation:** The first step in the motor task analysis of the skill will be to break the skill into continuous steps. Each step needs to involve a distinct skill to master the particular skill. After that, detailed analysis of the component parts and progression can be performed.

## QUESTION 6

I. Ensure the ball is close to the feet
II. Remain in a slightly crouched position
III. Use only the dominant foot for better control

Which of the above should a player attempt to do when dribbling a soccer ball in a restricted space?

A. I only
B. II only
C. I and II
D. I and III

**Answer:** C

**Explanation:** Both feet should be used when practicing dribbling. Ensuring the ball is close to the feet and remaining in a slightly crouched position are important when attempting to dribble a soccer ball in a restricted space.

## QUESTION 7

_____ is a locomotor skill where a foot finishes two tasks before the weight is passed on to the other foot.

    A. Running
    B. Jogging
    C. Skipping
    D. Walking

**Answer:** C

**Explanation:** When someone is skipping, each foot both walks and hops before the other foot takes over.

## QUESTION 8

Martin is a swimmer, and during practice, he maintains a straight body with the legs near the surface. This results in:

    A. reducing the drag from the water on Martin
    B. decreasing Martin's speed during swimming
    C. increasing Martin's buoyancy
    D. increasing the potential energy on Martin

**Answer:** A

**Explanation:** Having a steady foil shape while swimming decreases the resistance of the water or drag on the moving body. Water is denser than air, so there is a lot of resistance to movement. Swimming with a hot body with the legs near the surface is the most efficient in increasing speed and reducing drag forces of the water on the moving body.

## QUESTION 9

Which of the following is true about the principle of gravity?

    A. a wider base of support is easier than a narrow base of support

    B. during a static balance the line of gravity should go through the base of the support

    C. leaning over the line of gravity should be countered with extension of the body part in opposite direction

    D. during a dynamic activity the line of gravity should go through the base of the support

**Answer:** A

**Explanation:** Center of gravity is lower, easier to balance. Increasing distance between feet increases base of support.

## QUESTION 10

    I.    located in the front, top half of the arm

    II.    function is to flex the elbow

    III.    used when carrying things

The above describes which part of the muscular system:

    A. abdominals

    B. biceps

    C. triceps

    D. pectorals

**Answer:** B

**Explanation:** Biceps are located in the front, top half of the arm, and one function is to flex the elbow. Biceps are used when carrying things.

## QUESTION 11

What muscle extends the elbow in an overhead throw?

    A. biceps

    B. triceps

    C. pectorals

    D. deltoids

**Answer:** A

**Explanation:** Biceps are the muscles that extend the elbow in an overhead throw.

## QUESTION 12

Which of the following activities is not appropriate for K-12 school physical education programs?

    A. volleyball

    B. dodgeball

    C. hockey

    D. climbing

**Answer:** B

**Explanation:** According to the National Association for Sports and Physical Education, dodgeball is not an appropriate activity for K-12 school physical education programs. The purpose of physical education is to provide students with:

- skills needed to be physically active for a lifetime
- activities that are connected to health benefits
- positive experiences

## QUESTION 13

Which of the following requires that students with disabilities receive specially designed physical education services, if necessary?

- A. IDEA 2004
- B. IDEA 2010
- C. IEP
- D. NASPE

**Answer:** A

**Explanation:** IDEA 2004 required that students with disabilities receive specially designed physical education services, if necessary.

## QUESTION 14

Before children learn how to properly skip, what locomotor skill should they learn?

- A. hopping
- B. galloping
- C. sliding
- D. kicking

**Answer:** B

**Explanation:** Skipping is basically an advanced form of galloping, so the first step in skipping is to know how to gallop.

## QUESTION 15

Which of the following is best first to learn when swimming?

    A. flutter kick
    B. whip kick
    C. breaststroke
    D. gliding

**Answer:** A

**Explanation:** Flutter kick is the most basic part of swimming and knowing how to do the flutter kick helps in staying afloat.

## QUESTION 16

In theory, when running, what is the proper direction the legs should be moving?

    A. back and forth
    B. up and down
    C. in a cycle
    D. sideways

**Answer:** C

**Explanation:** In theory, the legs should be moving like a cycle; a bicycle wheel.

## QUESTION 17

When individuals are constantly involved in resistance weight training, they are likely to benefit the body by:

- A. decreasing chances of heart disease
- B. increasing bone density
- C. increasing blood flow
- D. decreasing joint dismemberment

**Answer:** B

**Explanation:** Resistance weight training applies active stress on the skeletal system, which leads to an increase in the density of long bones. This occurs because of an increase in mineral deposition into the bone matrix.

## QUESTION 18

What does the sergeant jump test measure?

- A. agility
- B. strength
- C. height
- D. speed

**Answer:** B

**Explanation:** Sergeant jump test is measurement of muscular strength and power of the lower body.

## QUESTION 19

     I.     cyclist's knees

    II.    swimmer's arms

   III.   runner's legs

Of the above, which of the following displays the concept of angular motion?

    A.  I only
    B.  I and II
    C.  I and III
    D.  I, II and III

**Answer:** D

**Explanation:** Angular motion can be defined as the motion of a body about a fixed axis. This concept is represented in all three options.

## QUESTION 20

Which of the following is most critical for the sport of golf?

    A.  agility
    B.  coordination
    C.  balance
    D.  speed

**Answer:** C

**Explanation:** Balance is essential to ensure a good golf swing. Maintaining the balance can deliver the clubhead to the ball with both speed and accuracy.

## QUESTION 21

    I.    motor learning

   II.    kinesiology

  III.    biomechanics

Of the above disciplines, which are the foundation(s) for physical education?

- A. I only
- B. I and II
- C. II and III
- D. I, II, and III

**Answer:** D

**Explanation:** Motor learning, motor development, kinesiology, biomechanics, exercise physiology, sport psychology, sport sociology, and aesthetics are all combined to create the foundation for physical education.

## QUESTION 22

In physical education lesson planning, there is a concern of liability. Which of the following is not a way to avoid negligence claims?

- A. Following procedures and practices that are addressed in national organization guidelines.
- B. Explaining new activities in detail to students prior to starting the activities.
- C. Ensuring students are properly and safely executing activities.
- D. Maintaining an active, ongoing process of supervision throughout activities.

**Answer:** B

**Explanation:** The best approach is to implement common activities, follow standards, ensure safety, and monitor students. Explaining innovative activities is not the best approach for avoid negligence claims.

**QUESTION 23**

Which of the following assessments is best used to assess the fitness f students with disabilities?

A. Fitnessgram
B. ActivityGram
C. President's Challenge
D. Brockport Physical Fitness Test

**Answer:** D

**Explanation:** The Brockport Physical Fitness Test (BPFT) is for youngsters with disabilities and designed to correspond as closely as possible to health-related, criterion-referenced tests for children without disability.

**QUESTION 24**

Swimming three-fourths of a mile three times a week is most likely to develop which of the following?

A. balance
B. agility
C. strength
D. aerobic fitness

**Answer:** D

**Explanation:** The long distance is best related to increase cardiovascular fitness, similar to distance running.

## QUESTION 25

Tennis player A had player B off balance and near the net, what kind of shot should player A perform?

    A.  backhand drive

    B.  lob

    C.  drop

    D.  forehand drive

**Answer:** B

**Explanation:** Playing B will have difficulty in returning a lob, if Player A chooses to lob the ball, because he or she is located near the net and is off balance.

## QUESTION 26

Having a third grade student use one leg and one hand to static balance is most useful for:

    A.  increasing strength

    B.  developing agility

    C.  increasing endurance

    D.  developing body awareness

**Answer:** D

**Explanation:** Practicing static balancing with one leg and one hand promotes students' identification and use of their body parts, which increases body awareness.

# QUESTION 27

_____ is a sub-discipline of physical education that focuses on the effects of various physical demands, particularly exercise, on the structure and function of the body.

    A.  Motor development

    B.  Exercise physiology

    C.  Exercise biomechanics

    D.  Exercise psychology

**Answer:** B

**Explanation:** Exercise physiology is a sub-discipline of physical education that focuses on the effects of various physical demands, particularly exercise, on the structure and function of the body.

# QUESTION 28

Which of the following is a similarity in physical education, exercise science, and sport?

    A.  aerobic activity

    B.  physical activity

    C.  aerobic activity

    D.  strength activity

**Answer:** B

**Explanation:** Physical education, exercise science, and sport all share physical activity.

## QUESTION 29

Which of the following is a goal of Healthy People 2010?

  A.  increase the graduation rate from junior high school
  B.  increase years of healthy life
  C.  eliminate health inconsistencies
  D.  both B and C

**Answer:** D

**Explanation:** Healthy People 2010 goals include increasing the years of healthy life and eliminating health inconsistencies.

## QUESTION 30

The back-saver sit and reach test is used to measure which of the following?

  A.  hamstring flexibility
  B.  trunk flexibility
  C.  lower back strength
  D.  upper back strength

**Answer:** A

**Explanation:** The back-saver sit and reach test primarily measures the flexibility of the hamstring muscles (one side at a time).

**QUESTION 31**

Which of the following groups' created around the 1840s and 1850s results in growth of physical education?

A. YMCA
B. NASPE
C. YWCA
D. SHAPE

**Answer:** A

**Explanation:** YMCA (Young Men's Christian Association) founding in June 1844 aims to put Christian principles into practice by developing a healthy "body, mind, and spirit".

**QUESTION 32**

Which of the following most likely results in enhancing an adolescent's sense of self-worth?

A. engaging in team activities in positive manner
B. working toward goals
C. implementing rules of games
D. creating new games and sports

**Answer:** A

**Explanation:** The keyword in the question is "self-worth". If individuals are working in a team and contributing in a positive manner, they will feel that they are a part of the team. This is related to feeling worthy of oneself.

## QUESTION 33

When constructing a test to assess students' knowledge at the completion of a unit on physical education foundation, which of the following is most critical for the assessment?

- A. to test students at the end of the activity
- B. to test content that is aligned to the defined learning goals of the unit
- C. to take into account students with learning disabilities
- D. to understand that not all students will have the same knowledge

**Answer:** B

**Explanation:** This assessment will be done at the end of the unit, so the assessment needs to be aligned to the learning goals of the unit. Taking into account students with learning disabilities is important, but not the most critical of the choices.

## QUESTION 34

At the end of a unit on soccer, Mr. Locke is seeking to determine what the students have learned. Which of the following assessments is the best to implement?

- A. authentic assessment
- B. standards-based assessment
- C. summative assessment
- D. norm-referenced assessment

**Answer:** C

**Explanation:** The goal of a summative assessment is to assess student learning at the end of an instructional unit by comparing it against some standards or objectives.

## QUESTION 35

Mr. Locke, a high school teacher, is teaching a foundational lesson on throwing a football. He knows that his students have a natural understanding of the topic going into it. He is intending to understand what they know before he begins the unit. He will use their prior knowledge to create activities to help them understand the concepts involved in throwing a football. Which of the following assessments is best for Mr. Locke?

- A. criterion-based assessment
- B. norms-based assessment
- C. formative assessment
- D. authentic assessment

**Answer:** C

**Explanation:** Mr. Locke is looking to understand prior knowledge to create an activity. He can administer a pre-assessment or a diagnostic test, which is within the category of formative assessments.

## QUESTION 36

Which of the following types of assessments includes a variety of samples of a student's work, collected overtime, that shows the student's growth and development?

- A. anecdotal records
- B. portfolio
- C. running record
- D. grades

**Answer:** B

**Explanation:** Portfolios include sample of student's works collected overtime. The portfolios show progression of student's growths and developments.

## QUESTION 37

      I.    a portfolio

      II.   an intelligence test

      III.  an adaptive behavior scale

Of the above, which of the following is/are formal assessment(s)?

A. I and II

B. I and III

C. II and III

D. I, II, and III

**Answer:** C

**Explanation:** A portfolio is an informal assessment. An intelligent test and adaptive behavior scale are formal assessments.

## QUESTION 38

A teacher is seeking to find out if students have mastered the instructional objectives at the end of a unit. What type of assessment is the best to use?

A. norm referenced

B. achievement

C. diagnostic

D. placement

**Answer:** B

**Explanation:** An achievement test is a test of developed skill or knowledge.

## QUESTION 39

Which of the following assessments is used to evaluate student learning at the conclusion of an instructional period (ex. at the end of a unit)?

    A. formative assessment
    B. interim assessment
    C. summative assessment
    D. placement assessment

**Answer:** C

**Explanation:** Summative assessment is used to evaluate student learning at the conclusion of an instructional period. Formative assessment is an in-process evaluation of learning that is normally administered multiple times during a unit or course. Placement assessment is used to place students in courses. Interim assessment is used to see if students are in the right track for learning.

## QUESTION 40

A middle school teacher is looking to use an informal assessment to capture overall learning. Which of the following is the best option?

    A. authentic assessment
    B. graded homework
    C. exit card
    D. performance assessment

**Answer:** C

**Explanation:** Of the answer choices, only an exit card is an informal assessment.

## QUESTION 41

Ongoing observation in authentic contexts with which the student is customary to and has had opportunities to practice is most appropriately used when assessing student's progress in

_____.

    A. physical education content knowledge
    B. motor performance
    C. team competition
    D. playing soccer

**Answer:** B

**Explanation:** Ongoing observation in authentic contexts with which the student is customary to and has had opportunities to practice is most appropriately used when assessing student's progress in motor performance areas.

## QUESTION 42

What reflex in children up to 5 years old can affect the gross motor skill of catching a ball?

    A. ball handling
    B. throwing
    C. kicking
    D. bending

**Answer:** A

**Explanation:** For children up to 5 years old, ball handling is gross motor skill of catching a ball that might be impacted.

**QUESTION 43**

A teacher walks in the room and a child is lying on the ground unconscious. What is the first action the teacher should take?

    A. remove any surrounding objects that might cause more harm to the student

    B. perform CPR

    C. leave the scene and call 911

    D. call the school nurse

**Answer:** B

**Explanation:** Option A and C do not help the student. Calling the nurse is not the priority. Teachers are trained to perform CPR, and the teacher should perform CPR.

**QUESTION 44**

Jenny's dad promised that he is going to attend the basketball game. However, he ended up having to go work. With the dad not showing up for the game, Jenny's _____ is most impacted.

    A. self-discipline

    B. self-esteem

    C. social interaction

    D. self-image

**Answer:** B

**Explanation:** Self-esteem is confidence in one's own worth or abilities. When the dad did not show up, that will impact Jenny's self-esteem.

**QUESTION 45**

What is the best warm-up for the front crawl in swimming?

A. dragging fingers along the top of the water and raising the elbow higher
B. running in shallow water
C. stretching and performing a warm up routine
D. practice keeping the body positioned flatly to be streamlined in the water

**Answer:** A

**Explanation:** To best be ready for the front crawl in swimming, the finger-tip drag is the best approach. On the recovery, drag the finger tips lightly across the water before entering for the next pull; this works on high elbow during recovery. Option is C is very vague. Option B is not the best approach for crawl swimming. Option D is a technique performed during the activity.

**QUESTION 46**

In track and field events, starting blocks are most commonly used in which event?

A. long jumps
B. distance running
C. running
D. sprints

**Answer:** D

**Explanation:** Sprinting is running over a short distance in a limited period of time. Individuals begin the race by getting in the crouching position in the starting blocks before leaning forward and gradually moving into an upright position

**QUESTION 47**

A 15-year-old student whose heart rate is 130 beats per minutes would be considered to be:

    A. at ventilatory threshold
    B. performing submaximal exercise
    C. performing maximal exercise
    D. hyperventilating

**Answer:** B

**Explanation:** For a normal physically-fit 15 year old, the target heart rate zone for maximal exercise is well above 140 beats per minutes. He is considered to be performing submaximal exercise.

**QUESTION 48**

Jimmy is looking to lose weight and build endurance, so the key target zone is 60% of his maximum heart rate. Jimmy is 30 years old. What is his maximum heart rate for the key target zone?

    A. 100
    B. 114
    C. 130
    D. 190

**Answer:** B

**Explanation:** Jimmy is 30 years old and his estimated maximum heart rate is 220-30=190. The maximum heart rate for his key target zone is his maximum heart rate times 0.6 ($190 \times 0.6$ =114).

## QUESTION 49

Medical attention is required when blood pressure becomes higher than:

    A.  180/110

    B.  145/90

    C.  120/80

    D.  150/100

**Answer:** A

**Explanation:** Blood pressure higher than 180/110 mm Hg requires immediate medical attention as a hypertensive crisis can occur.

## QUESTION 50

The moment of inertia is greatest when more mass is at a _____ distance from the axis of rotation.

    A.  lesser

    B.  greater

    C.  equal

    D.  center

**Answer:** B

**Explanation:** The moment of inertia is greatest when more mass is at a greater distance from the axis of rotation.

## QUESTION 51

Which of the following causes possible excessive vomiting, tremors, sweating and anxiety?

    A. stimulants

    B. depressants

    C. painkillers

    D. anabolic steroids

**Answer:** A

**Explanation:** Stimulants cause possible excessive vomiting, tremors, sweating and anxiety. Examples of stimulants include adderall, ritalin, dexedrine, and benzedrine.

## QUESTION 52

Which of the following is the best reflective assessment for a group of elementary education students learning about basics of soccer?

    A. Ask students to think about what they learned, and then write out their reflection in a sentence with "I learned …."

    B. Ask students to complete a worksheet that has questions related to the content presented to them.

    C. Ask students to write down key concepts during reflective assessment.

    D. Ask students to draw what they remember about the content presented to them.

**Answer:** A

**Explanation:** A reflective assessment is when students can experience an assessment as a part of learning, rather than as a separate evaluative process. Having students think about what they learned and write it down is example of reflective assessment best for elementary education students.

## QUESTION 53

Which of the following societies stands for health and physical education?

    A. SHAPE
    B. NATA
    C. NCCEA
    D. NECA

**Answer:** A

**Explanation:** SHAPE stands for Society of Health and Physical Education.

## QUESTION 54

Emily stretched her ligaments in her calf, which is considered a

    A. strain
    B. sprain
    C. heat cramp
    D. stress

**Answer:** A

**Explanation:** Ligaments are a short band of tough, flexible, fibrous connective tissue that connects two bones or cartilages or holds together a joint. When Emily stretched her ligaments in her calf, she experienced a calf strain, which is a tear in one or more of the calf muscles at the back of the lower leg.

## QUESTION 55

Which of the following has the most caffeine?

    A. 8 oz coffee
    B. 8 oz tea
    C. 12 oz soda
    D. a chocolate bar

**Answer:** A

**Explanation:** An 8 oz coffee has more caffeine than any of the other choices.

**QUESTION 56**

To improve his kicking skills for soccer, Drew's trainer recommended that he train with a leg-extension exercise, along with gradually increasing its weight to increase his strength. The leg extension exercise works the _____ muscle.

    A. trapezius

    B. hamstring

    C. gluteus maximus

    D. quadriceps

**Answer:** D

**Explanation:** The quadricep is the large muscle at the front of the thigh, which is divided into four distinct portions and acts to extend the leg.

**QUESTION 57**

In football, a player should extend his or her kicking leg when contacting a football during a punt. Which of the following is the best reason for undertaking such a move?

    A. to allow for greater distance and time to apply the force to the football with the kicking foot

    B. to increase the radius from the axis of rotation, the hip joint, which results in the kicking foot moving faster than any other part of the leg on contact

    C. to reduce the force of interaction between the kicking foot and the ball

    D. to lessen the reaction of the force being exerted and decrease the flexing of the leg

**Answer:** B

**Explanation:** This increases the chance of distance and accuracy and also limits the threat of an injury.

**QUESTION 58**

A physical education instructor in her swimming class is telling her fifth grade students to point toes like a diver, kick heels, and roll chin to shoulder. The teacher's intention is most likely to help the students swim more effectively by:

A. encouraging teamwork
B. placing less stress on the knees
C. reducing the effects of drag by the water movement
D. increasing energy during activity

**Answer:** C

**Explanation:** Drag of water creates a lot of stress. The key is to minimize that stress, which is done by what the instructer is informing her fifth grade students. The physical education instructor would do this because pointing toes like a diver, kicking heels, and rolling the chin to the shoulder would reduce the effects of drag by the water movement by giving the body the best possible chance to move through the water.

## QUESTION 59

During physical education class, a group of third-graders see that some students are better at balancing, some are better at tumbling, and some are better at jumping. As a result, the teacher informs the students that everyone is good at different things and everybody can improve with practice. The teacher's response to her class shows that the teacher's awareness of the role of physical education is:

    A.  establishing competition as students see different level of skills
    B.  teaching awareness and respect for diverse talents and abilities
    C.  ensuring all students get a opportunities to improve
    D.  promoting students' integration via of nonlocomotor and locomotor skills.

**Answer:** B

**Explanation:** All students have different abilities, and students need to understanding that, at an early age, so they can be better team players. By informing the students that everyone is good at different things, the teacher is showing respect for diverse talents and abilities.

## QUESTION 60

Which of the following best describes activities that will increase the cardio-respiratory capacity and includes dynamic stretches?

    A.  low-intensity aerobic activities
    B.  moderate-intensity aerobic activities
    C.  high-intensity aerobic activities
    D.  none of the above

**Answer:** B

**Explanation:** Low-intensity activities will not increase cardio-respiratory capacity nor will high-intensity aerobic activities. Moderate-intensity aerobic activities will increase the cardio-respiratory capacity.

**QUESTION 61**

A physical education teacher is looking to incorporate biomechanical concepts in her classroom as part of cross curriculum. The teacher wants to ensure students understand the application of static and dynamic balance skills. To ensure state standards of cross curriculum are satisfied, which of the following biomechanical concepts can be best implemented in her lesson?

    A. kinetic energy

    B. potential energy

    C. center of gravity

    D. centripetal force

**Answer:** C

**Explanation:** Cross curriculum is when introducing another subject area into the lesson. The physical education teacher can bring the physics concept of center of gravity, which is related to static and dynamic balance skills.

**QUESTION 62**

As individuals develop, the hypothalamus signals the pituitary gland to release growth hormone and causes the production of thyroxine, resulting in gains in body size and skeletal growth. The increase in this substance is a result primarily o f what two body systems interaction?

    A. skeletal system and muscular system

    B. skeletal system and nervous system

    C. respiratory system and skeletal system

    D. nervous system and endocrine system

**Answer:** D

**Explanation:** The increase in thyroxine is due to the hypothalamus signaling the pituitary gland to release growth hormone. The keywords are "signals" and "hormone". The nervous system is associated with signals while endocrine system is associated with hormone. Body size and skeletal growth are linked to Option A, but the question is asking for the reason in increase of thyroxine instead of the reason for the resulting effect.

QUESTION 63

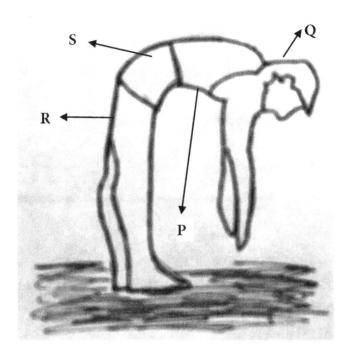

In the above image, which of the following locates the center of gravity?

    E.  Q
    F.  P
    G. R
    H. S

**Answer:** D

**Explanation:** The center of gravity is the average location of the weight of an object. This is best indicated by option D.

## QUESTION 64

Pushing, bouncing, circling, and twisting are best described as?

- A. locomotors skills
- B. specialized skills
- C. nonlocomotor skills
- D. manipulative skills

**Answer:** C

**Explanation:** Locomotors movements are things like running and skipping. They are movements resulting in moving from one point to another. Nonlocomotor movements occur in the body parts or the whole body and do not cause the body to travel.

## QUESTION 65

Standard 2 of the National Standards for Physical Education states the following: "Demonstrates understanding of movement concepts, principles, strategies, and tactics as they apply to the learning and performance of physical activities." Of the following which does not display Standard 2?

- A. During soccer practice, the teacher tells the students to place their nonkicking feet alongside the ball to create velocity in their kicking feet.
- B. The teacher tells students to bring the ball back behind their heads with their elbows bent to increase the distance throw.
- C. The teacher tells the students to use their heads for ball movement.
- D. The teacher tells students to flex their tuck and tend their arms with strength and directly overhead on the release.

**Answer:** C

**Explanation:** Option A, B, and D all are connected to Standard 2 of movement concepts, principles, strategies, and tactics. Option C is not displaying the purpose of Standard 2.

**QUESTION 66**

| | Word | Definition |
|---|---|---|
| I | Muscular Strength | the ability of the muscle to continue to perform without fatigue. |
| II | Muscular Endurance | the maximum amount of force a muscle can produce in a single effort. |
| III | Body Composition | the ratio of lean tissue to fat tissue in the body. |
| IV | Cardio Respiratory Endurance | the ability of the circulatory and respiratory systems to supply oxygen during sustained physical activity. |

In the above table, which of the following is incorrectly defined?

    A. I only
    B. II only
    C. I and II
    D. II, III, and IV

 **Answer:** C

**Explanation:** Body composition is defined as the proportion of fat and muscle in an individual's body. Muscular endurance is when a muscle or group of muscles repeatedly exert force against resistance; it is more than a single effort. Muscular strength is the maximum amount of force that a muscle can exert against some form of resistance in a single effort. Cardio respiratory endurance is the heart's and lung's ability to absorb, transfer, and utilize oxygen during extended physical exertion. The circulatory system is to supply oxygen to the body, not just to both the respiratory and circular system.

**QUESTION 67**

Which of the following correctly defines balance, time, force, and flow?

   A.

   Balance: Understand the nature of static and dynamic balance and the role of balance in movement.
   Time: Differentiate among speeds and to increase or decrease the speed of movement.
   Force: To be able to create and modify one's force to meet the demands of the task
   Flow: To combine movements smoothly and to perform movements within a restricted time or space

   B.

   Balance: Differentiate among speeds and to increase or decrease the speed of movement.
   Time: Understand the nature of static and dynamic balance and the role of balance in movement.
   Force: To be able to create and modify one's force to meet the demands of the task
   Flow: To combine movements smoothly and to perform movements within a restricted time or space

   C.

   Balance: Differentiate among speeds and to increase or decrease the speed of movement.
   Time: Understand the nature of static and dynamic balance and the role of balance in movement.
   Force: To combine movements smoothly and to perform movements within a restricted time or space .
   Flow: To be able to create and modify one's force to meet the demands of the task

   D.

   Balance: To combine movements smoothly and to perform movements within a restricted time or space.
   Time: Differentiate among speeds and to increase or decrease the speed of movement.
   Force: To be able to create and modify one's force to meet the demands of the task
   Flow: Understand the nature of static and dynamic balance and the role of balance in movement.

**Answer:** A

**Explanation:** Option A correctly defines balance, time, force, and flow.

**QUESTION 68**

Which of the following is not a non-locomotor movement?

    A.  lifting

    B.  rotating

    C.  jogging

    D.  flexing

**Answer:** C

**Explanation:** Lifting, rotating, and flexing are all non-locomotor skills while jogging is a locomotor skill.

**QUESTION 69**

A physical education teacher instructs a student to push his elbow toward his chest and hold the stretch for 20 seconds. Which of the following muscles are being targeted here?

    A.  brachialis

    B.  deltoid

    C.  latissimus

    D.  rotator cuff

**Answer:** B

**Explanation:** The deltoid is the muscle being targeted because it is the located near where the stretching is happening.

**QUESTION 70**

Aerial tumbling moves require safety precautions. Which of the following safety precautions is most critical in practicing flips and somersaults?

A. wearing proper equipment
B. having qualified spotters
C. using triple-thickness mats
D. practice slowly prior to going full force

**Answer:** B

**Explanation:** Having qualified spotters is the most critical component when practicing flips and somersaults because a watcher is needed in situations where someone is falling while practicing.

**QUESTION 71**

A physical education teacher has constructed an activity where students will walk in and around large hoop placed on the floor. This activity is most useful in developing which of the following fundamental skills?

A. spatial awareness
B. rhythmic movement
C. static balance
D. locomotive skills

**Answer:** A

**Explanation:** The activity where students will walk in and around large hoop placed on the floor will develop self-control of surrounding, in which students control on where they place their feet.

**QUESTION 72**

Matt sees a flyer for a weight-loss pill that states the pill can cause someone to lose 15 pounds in only 7 days. The flyer says that the pill is all natural and healthy. Which of the following is the best action for Curtis to take to make sure that this product is safe to use?

    A. compare the advertisements of different weight losing pills
    B. complete an online research on the pill and company offering the pill
    C. start a diet while taking the weight-loss pill
    D. ask a friend about the product

**Answer:** B

**Explanation:** Doing independent online research on the pill and the company offering the pill is the best approach to ensure the product is safe and reliable to use.

## QUESTION 73

A tenth grade student desires to improve cardio-respiratory endurance along with reducing body fat. The student has decided to implement the following plan:

Frequency of Workout: 7 days a week

Intensity of Workout: Moderate

Work out Details:

I.    Warm-up (20 minutes): Jogging in place with dynamic stretching
II.    Cycling for 40 minutes
III.    Cool down (15 minutes): Walking with flexibility exercises

Which of the following modification will best help to ensure the student's goal is achieved?

A. increase the time of teaching activity by 10 minutes
B. add several components related to resistance or weight training
C. implement robust exercise activities
D. implement the plan outlined in the mornings and nights

**Answer:** B

**Explanation:** The student should add weight training because weight training burns more fat than just doing cardio.

## QUESTION 74

    I.    to respond readily to instructions

    II.    to follow rules, codes, and safety practices

    III.    to work with other students to ensure learning

    IV.    to warm up and recover from exercise

Which of the following are ways to teach students on ensuring safe practices are being implemented in physical education classrooms?

    A.  I and II

    B.  II and III

    C.  I, II, and IV

    D.  II, III, and IV

**Answer:** C

**Explanation:** Working with other students to ensure learning is not related to ensuring safe practices occurs in physical education classrooms. All other options have a connection to ensuring safety in physical education classrooms.

## QUESTION 75

As a physical education teacher, promoting health education is a central responsibility. A physical education teacher is communicating the negatives of smoking while the teacher has the habit of smoking. Another physical education teacher is prompting healthy eating, while noticeably overweight. These physical education teachers are implementing which type of communication?

    A.  verbal communication

    B.  non-verbal communication

    C.  contradicting messages

    D.  unintentional communication

**Answer:** B

**Explanation:** The teachers are using non-verbal communication as a way to communicate contradicting messages. The question is asking for the type of communication, and "contradicting messages" is not a form of communication.

## QUESTION 76

Engaging the entire family in a healthy eating plan is most likely the best approach in which of the following?

    A. Supporting elementary students to eating healthy.

    B. Supporting an adolescent in losing weight.

    C. Teaching kids on importance of eating healthy.

    D. Supporting state curriculum of teaching healthy eating at home.

**Answer:** B

**Explanation:** Engaging the whole family is the best approach in supporting the adolescent to lose weight because the student lives with their family most of the time and the family can encourage them to lose weight.

## QUESTION 77

Which of the following activities is considered a true net/wall game?

    A. badminton

    B. hiking

    C. lacrosse

    D. soccer

**Answer:** A

**Explanation:** Badminton is considered a true net/wall game because it is the only answer that requires a net to play.

## QUESTION 78

In school classes, folk dances for grade K-12 are best when emphasizing:

A. polka steps
B. tinkling steps
C. locomotor skills
D. manipulative skills

**Answer:** C

**Explanation:** Folk dances are best when emphasizing locomotor skills because of the movement associated with dancing.

## QUESTION 79

Which of the following is the best way to learn about the best practices to start teaching physical education during first year of instructing?

A. Give students a survey on the teaching methods being implemented in the classroom, so teachers obtain feedback on improvement.
B. Observe lessons taught by an experienced physical education teachers and note the types of activity in which there are involved, their sequence, and the time spent on the lesson.
C. Undergo yearly professional training on teaching methods for physical education curriculum.
D. Set monthly meetings with principals or mentors on obtaining feedback on teaching.

**Answer:** B

**Explanation:** The best way to learn the best practices is to observe lessons being taught by experienced physical education teacher because they will know more on how to correctly instruct the students. Observing also provides an opportunity to ask questions in real time to the experienced physical education teacher.

**QUESTION 80**

  I.  balance

  II.  speed

  III.  strength

  IV.  coordination

Agility is the ability to change the direction of the body in an efficient and effective manner. To achieve this, which of the following is required?

  A. I and II

  B. I, II, and III

  C. I, III, and IV

  D. I, II, III, and IV

**Answer:** D

**Explanation:** Balance is the ability to maintain equilibrium when stationary or moving. Speed is the ability to move all or part of the body quickly. Strength is the ability to overcome a resistance. Coordination is the ability to control the movement of the body. To achieve agility, balance, speed, strength, and coordination are needed.

## QUESTION 81

Once a physical education instructor has taught a lesson or part of a lesson, and before the thinking of planning the next lesson, instructor needs to evaluate the effectiveness of the current lesson. Which of the following reasons is not correct for undertaking this approach?

A. Essential part of capturing student learning along with instructor learning and ensure progress of student.
B. To document student progress to be able to make comparison analysis of student progress.
C. Ensure objectives of the lesson were achieved, but also whether the objectives were, in fact, realistic and appropriate.
D. To support instructor in developing future lesson.

**Answer:** B

**Explanation:** Evaluating the effectiveness of the current lesson is to capture student learning, ensure objectives are achieved, and support in developing future lessons.

## QUESTION 82

A physical education teacher has an instructional unit on basketball that addresses basic dribbling, passing, and shooting skills along with techniques such as drills, partner work, and modified games. Half the course is often used with the basket typically lowered below the regulation height. This instructional unit best describes which grade level?

A. second grade
B. fourth grade
C. eight grade
D. night grade

**Answer:** B

**Explanation:** The lesson is too basic for 8th or 9th grade students, and the lesson is too advanced for second grade students. The lesson is best suited for a fourth grade class.

## QUESTION 83

The following diagram shows a process an instructor uses to monitor movements in physical activities.

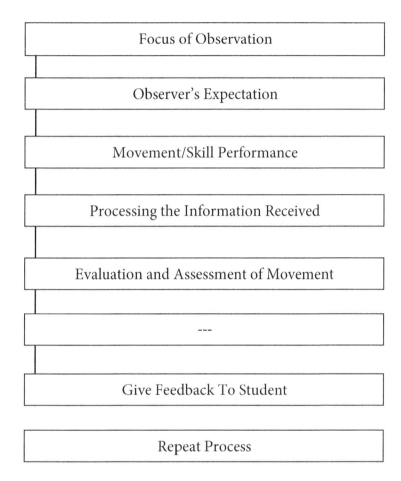

Which of the following is best to place in the blank box above?

A. Document assessment in grade book
B. Compare results with other classroom students
C. Evaluate effectiveness of assessment
D. Priorities and plan feedback

**Answer:** D

**Explanation:** Prior to giving the feedback, the best approach is to priorities which feedback is critical to communication and plan how to give the feedback.

## QUESTION 84

Various forms of assessments are used in the physical education classroom. Assessments that allow ongoing feedback to progress toward skill learning goals are called:

A. summative assessments
B. formative assessments
C. formal assessments
D. informal assessments

**Answer:** B

**Explanation:** The form of assessment that allows for ongoing feedback to progress toward skill learning goals is called the formative assessment.

## QUESTION 85

Which of the following is best describes a formal assessment?

A. performing a standardized skill test from a sport (such as a kicking a soccer ball to make a goal)
B. observing players passing the ball in a game and remembering the level of passing performance
C. using a list to assess performance in a game
D. using a scale to assess performance in a game

**Answer:** A

**Explanation:** Performing a standardized skill test from a sport is the best way to show a formal assessment.

## QUESTION 86

During a creative arts seminar, several juggling stations are set up that are devoted to the physical education department. Different objects such as scarves, balls, beanbags and small plastic hoops are available. Students may move to different stations at will and may juggle with multiple objects. Which of the following is primary advantage of this type of setup?

- A.  it displays to everyone that physical education involves multiple activities and cross curriculum
- B.  it minimizes the possibility that students will get bored
- C.  it gives students choices in deciding entry levels into the activity
- D.  it gives students the opportunity to think which activity is hardest to complete

**Answer:** C

**Explanation:** The juggling station allows for different levels of entry because there are different stations that a student can start from. The different stations allow the students to select which one to start with.

## QUESTION 87

The Fitnessgram physical fitness assessment program places its highest priority on:

- A.  comparing student scores within the same age group
- B.  helping school children to be active
- C.  developing health-related behaviors to be attained by students
- D.  high fitness performance

**Answer:** C

**Explanation:** The Fitnessgram assessment places its highest priority on the development of health-related behaviors to be attained by the students.

**QUESTION 88**

The goal of a secondary physical education program is to prompt the value of teamwork and teach cooperative skills. Which of the following activities will support the goal of the secondary physical education school program?

    A. In a soccer game, have students who are rotated out of the game to support teammates with positive comments.

    B. In a soccer game, have students focus on passing while simultaneously playing their own positions in practice games.

    C. Have students select teammates at the start of the school year and have them work with the same teammates throughout the school year.

    D. Pair students who lag in physical activities to those who are progressing in a positive direction toward the goal.

**Answer:** B

**Explanation:** In soccer games, having students focus on passing while simultaneously playing their own positions in practice games supports the goal of secondary education by involving all the students.

**QUESTION 89**

Which of the following are responsible for controlling muscular movement of the head, neck, body and limbs and transmitting the nerve impulses to the central nervous system after receiving a signal respectively?

    A. sympathetic nerve; parasympathetic nerve
    B. central nerve; autonomic nerve
    C. parasympathetic nerve; central nerve
    D. motor nerve; sensory nerve

**Answer:** D

**Explanation:** The motor nerve and sensory nerve are responsible for controlling muscular movement of the head, neck, body, and limbs because they are the nerves that help move those body parts.

## QUESTION 90

| Week | Sets | Repetitions | Load (kg) | Rest (s) |
|------|------|-------------|-----------|----------|
| 1 | 2 | 10 | 60 | 40 |
| 2 | 3 | 12 | 65 | 35 |
| 3 | 4 | 14 | 70 | 30 |

Which of the following training principle is best illustrated in the above program?

    A. specificity
    B. reversibility
    C. variance
    D. overload

**Answer:** D

**Explanation:** The training principle of overload is displayed in the above program because the weight is going up and the repetitions are increasing.

## QUESTION 91

    I.    To maintain aerobic fitness.
    II.    To maintain muscular strength.
    III.    To ease the psychological stress of the sprinter.

Which of the following are the reasons why a sprinter frequently uses ball games in the training program during off-season?

    A. I and II
    B. I and III
    C. II and III
    D. I, II, and III

**Answer:** A

**Explanation:** A sprinter would use aerobic fitness and muscular strength in the off-season because those would keep their body ready to perform rigorously.

**QUESTION 92**

The ratio of one's muscle, bone and body fat to one's body weight would be an example of his/her

    A. flexibility
    B. muscular endurance
    C. body composition
    D. muscular strength

**Answer:** C

**Explanation:** The ratio of one's muscle, bone, and body fat to one's body weight would be an example of body composition.

**QUESTION 93**

A concentric contraction causes muscles to shorten, thereby generating which of the following?

    A. sounds
    B. bonds
    C. forces
    D. distance

**Answer:** C

**Explanation:** A concentric contraction causes muscles to shorten, thereby generating force because flexing of the muscles is happening.

**QUESTION 94**

Which of the following hormones is produced more during the sleep cycle?

  A.  melatonin
  B.  somatostatin
  C.  thyrotropin
  D.  adrenaline

**Answer:** A

**Explanation:** Melatonin's primary function in the body is to regulate night and day cycles or sleep-wake cycles. Darkness causes the body to produce more melatonin, which indicates the body to prepare for sleep.

**QUESTION 95**

  I.    Shortened attention span
  II.   Decreased overall cognitive performance
  III.  Ineffective at self control
  IV.   Unable to achieve academically

Iron is a dietary mineral that is critical for various bodily functions, including the transport of oxygen in the blood. Which of the following is/are signs of iron deficiency in students?

  A.  I, II and III
  B.  I, II, and IV
  C.  I, III, and IV
  D.  II, III, and IV

**Answer:** B

**Explanation:** Iron deficiency is a condition of too little iron in the body. Signs showing iron deficiency include shortened attention span, decreased cognitive performance, and unable to achieve academically.

**QUESTION 96**

Nutrition, weight control, understanding muscular movement, and controlling postures are components of which of the following?

    A.  physical education

    B.  wellness

    C.  healthy eating

    D.  health education

**Answer:** B

**Explanation:** Nutrition, weight control, understanding muscular movement, and controlling postures are components of wellness.

**QUESTION 97**

Fitness plans that call for slowly adding weights or increasing resistance with each workout are called _____.

    A.  slow resistance

    B.  overload resistance

    C.  steady resistance

    D.  progressive resistance

**Answer:** C

**Explanation:** The training plan is called steady resistance because the weight is going steadily up and increasing with each workout.

**QUESTION 98**

What does sodium help regulate?

    A. muscles

    B. heart

    C. lungs

    D. eyes

Answer: A

Explanation: Sodium helps control blood pressure and regulates the function of muscles and nerves.

**QUESTION 99**

Body converts calories from food to energy. This is called _____.

    A. metabolism

    B. nutrition

    C. energy conservation

    D. all the above

**Answer:** A

**Explanation:** The body converts calories to food energy through metabolism because the body is metabolizing food into energy.

**QUESTION 100**

Piaget suggests which of the following is/are the basis for all intellectual functioning for approximately the first 2 years of life?

    A.  sensory experiences

    B.  motor experiences

    C.  sensory and motor experiences

    D.  motor and cognitive development

**Answer:** C

**Explanation:** Piaget suggests that the sensory and motor experiences are the basis for all intellectual function for approximately the first two years. Most people, in the first two years of their life, can sense and move around for the most part as they are in the learning stages.

## QUESTION 101

Prior to the start of school, a physical education teacher sends a letter home informing parents of upcoming lessons on the topic of sexuality. In the letter sent, the learning goals and objectives of the lesson are described. Regulations in states give parents or guardians the right to:

A. inform the school not to instruct the lesson to the child
B. attend the lesson to ensure the lesson is aligned with the letter provided
C. review the material prior to the lesson to decide if any information needs to be omitted
D. request to defer the lesson to a future school year

**Answer:** A

**Explanation:** Regulations in states give the parent or guardian the right to inform the school not to instruct the lesson to the child.

## QUESTION 102

When adapting activities for physical education, classmates can use the buddy system to do which of the following to help students with hearing impairments?

A. start
B. stop
C. relay information
D. all of these

**Answer:** D

**Explanation:** Individuals with hearing difficulties will benefit from a buddy system in starting, stopping, and gaining information.

**QUESTION 103**

Cerebral palsy and spina bifida/hydrocephalus are neurological disorders. What factor is the most critical to understand the effect on children's motor learning?

    A. see if family members have the same learning disorder
    B. see if the student has cognitive and physical challenges to learning
    C. see if the student has impairment issues
    D. see if the student is having difficulty completing assignments.

**Answer:** B

**Explanation:** As indicated in the question, cerebral palsy and spina bifida/hydrocephalus are neurological disorders, which can impact cognitive thinking, resulting in physical challenging.

**QUESTION 104**

A critical aspect of teaching physical education is having understanding of the influential factors. Of the following, which of the following is incorrect?

    A. Family situation and economic circumstances have impact on student learning.
    B. Different cultural groups may value different traditions, impacting the learning of motor skills.
    C. Environmental factor is sole impact on difference in performance of students.
    D. Various factors contribution to how students learn motor skills.

**Answer:** C

**Explanation:** One factor cannot be the impact of differences in performance of students.

## QUESTION 105

Which of the following explains how the distance and accuracy is increased, when throwing a Frisbee® by snapping the wrist sharply at the end of the throw?

    A. As the disk is thrown, additional kinetic energy is imparted which results in a farther throw.
    B. As the disk is thrown, it acts as a gyroscope and the stability is increased during the travel.
    C. As the disk is thrown, the sharp wrist movement causes conversion from static to dynamic movement.
    D. As the disk is thrown, there is a greater coefficient of friction, which reduces the drag between the disk and the air.

**Answer:** B

**Explanation:** The Frisbee acts as a gyroscope and the stability increases during travel because by snapping the wrist at the end of the throw makes the Frisbee spin faster, cutting through the air at a better rate.

## QUESTION 106

Which of the following displays appropriate application of the physiological principle of specificity, when planning physical education activities?

    A. Having students work in groups of four each week with different members each week.
    B. Having students complete activities that target muscle groups or energy systems that will support them in other class work.
    C. Allowing students to select class activities that interest them and rotating with teacher selected activities.
    D. Ensuring that lessons implemented in the classroom are tailored to the appropriate developmental and age level of the student

**Answer:** B

**Explanation:** Specificity is the principle of training that indicates what is done in the gym should be relevant and appropriate to a desired outcome. Choice B indicates the activity is to improve muscle groups or energy systems. The activities are important and there is a desired outcome, so Choice B is the only one related to the physiological principle of specificity.

**QUESTION 107**

    I.    common purpose and a commitment to achieve goals

    II.    opportunity for personal growth and social interaction

    III.    career opportunities are possible with interaction

Which of the following supports the idea that improving an adolescent's sense of self-worth is accomplished by working in team activities and having a positive contribution?

    A. I and II

    B. I and III

    C. II and III

    D. I, II, and III

**Answer:** A

**Explanation:** Having a common purpose and commitment to reach goals are important for working in team activities. Positive contribution is related to personal growth. In team activities, social interaction is needed to have positive contribution.

**QUESTION 108**

In a fourth grade classroom, individuals are working in groups to develop short original dance sequences for an upcoming school activity day. The physical education teacher gives each group a set of flashcards that has the following words:

jump – leap – slide – rocking step – turn – spin – collapse – balance – explode …

The requirement given to the students is to include those types of movements in their dances. By undertaking this approach, the physical education teacher is mostly improving student understanding of:

A. how dance can express how others are feeling in the classroom and make comparisons between movement
B. the role of dance composition in achieving creative expression along with the choreographic elements of dance
C. how to work with groups in cross curriculum activities to accomplish goals
D. different types of dance movements within different categories and periods in history

**Answer:** B

**Explanation:** There is nothing about movement mentioned in the question, so option A and D are eliminated. Individuals are working in groups, but the purpose is not to improve how to work in groups. The teacher is wanting to improve student understanding of the role of dance composition in achieving creative expression along with the choreographic elements of dance.

**QUESTION 109**

All of the following are benefits of a coaching career EXCEPT:

    A. work with skilled and motivated individuals
    B. the excitement of progressing
    C. demanding time commitment to prepare for games
    D. intrinsic rewards of respect

**Answer:** C

**Explanation:** Having to work long hours to get ready for games is not a benefit of coaching.

**QUESTION 110**

A group of seventh grade students are taking a high-ropes course after school. In doing so, the course involves climbing a rope ladder to a tree platform along with walking on a cable stretched between two trees. Which of the following is the best approach to ensure that the students are safe as they undertake this activity?

    A. conduct a group meeting on the activity that is going to be completed and the safety aspects that need to be taken into consideration
    B. ensure that the students wear a harness connected to an effective restraining system
    C. ensure that a supervisor is available onsite to monitor the activities and that emergency contact numbers are available
    D. complete the activity using ropes but with only fewer feet from the ground as a test prior to undertaking the full activity

**Answer:** B

**Explanation:** The students are involved in climbing a rope ladder to a platform, so the best safeguarding measure is to ensure that the students wear a harness connected to an effective restraining system.

## QUESTION 111

A group of high school students are planning to go rock climbing during the early part of the summer along with running a marathon during the latter part of the summer. Completing these two activities will most likely provide what benefit to the students?

- A. improve teamwork skills
- B. improve health
- C. improve self-image
- D. improve leadership skills

**Answer:** C

**Explanation:** Rock climbing and running a marathon are huge accomplishments for high school students. Completing these activities will improve self-image.

## QUESTION 112

Of the following, where should equipment for daily lessons be placed?

- A. away from students during attendance
- B. around perimeter of the gym
- C. back of the gym
- D. in center of the gym

**Answer:** B

**Explanation:** Having equipment around the perimeter of the gym makes it accessible and provides a safe environment.

**QUESTION 113**

A teacher is going to have students complete a new physical education activity. Of the following, which situation will most likely leave the teacher open to legal liability, if a student were injured during the activity?

A. Having students complete an activity outside of their capability.
B. Neglecting to inform students about safety issues and precautions related to the activity.
C. Neglecting to inform students of the plan prior to starting activity and resulting in an injury.
D. Focusing on one student while others are playing, ultimately resulting in an injury.

**Answer:** B

**Explanation:** In physical education classes, safety is critical to ensure that students go home the way they came to school. Not informing the students of safety issues and precautions can leave the teacher open to legal liability.

**QUESTION 114**

A third grade physical education teacher has students practice different locomotors skills through a unique game of tag in which students become either a snake or frog. The teacher assigns each animal type a different movement pattern and a type of prey to pursue. After being captured, an animal becomes the original species as the predator until eventually all students are the same species. Of the following, which is a best way to show the primary way that this locomotors activity builds competence in the affective domain?

A. by giving a fun, safe opportunity to practice playing a game following the rules
B. by giving students the chance to increase knowledge in movement skills
C. by giving students an opportunity to see how individual contribution can impact group accomplishments
D. by giving students a non-competitive gave in a physically safe atmosphere

**Answer:** A

**Explanation:** The game is low-organized, fun, and noncompetitive, so the environment is positive and safe. This is related to the affective domain. The games consist of rules, so that promotes students development of cooperative behaviors.

**QUESTION 115**

A first grade student is having trouble throwing a basketball into the modified net in the gym. Which of the following modifications would be most appropriate for this student?

    A.  modify the net
    B.  replace the ball with a smaller ball
    C.  have student use a lighter ball
    D.  decrease the distance of the student from the net

**Answer:** C

**Explanation:** The net is already modified, so Option A is not the answer. Using a lighter ball will allow the student to exert more force, improving student's ability to throw.

**QUESTION 116**

Smoking, poor nutrition, inactive, and excessive sleeping are examples of what form of health risk factors?

    A.  physical fitness
    B.  biological factors
    C.  inherited factors
    D.  behavioral factors

**Answer:** D

**Explanation:** All these factors are individuals choices, so the risk factors are behavioral related.

## QUESTION 117

Physical education activities need to be modified for individuals with physical disabilities. In a game of bowling, what is the best way to modify the game to accommodate individuals with physical disabilities?

- A. use lighter pins to allow the movement of pins
- B. use a ramp for rolling the ball
- C. use fewer pins
- D. give additional number of rolls

**Answer:** B

**Explanation:** Choice B supports a student with physical disabilities to be better involved in bowling.

## QUESTION 118

A physical education teacher teaching a golf unit observes that one of her top student is having difficulty with techniques despite continued coaching. The physical education teacher is aware of an upcoming exhibition of a golf match. The teacher encourages the student to attend the event. By providing this encouragement the teacher is most likely intending to take advantage of which of the following learning concepts?

- A. learning motor skills  via experiences individuals
- B. learning via observation
- C. learning via multimedia techniques
- D. learning via external means

**Answer:** A

**Explanation:** Experienced individuals will be involved in the exhibition, so the students can discuss and watch experienced golfers to improve their skills.

**QUESTION 119**

Of the following applications of technology, which will be best to help a wrestler learn a new take down technique?

    A. reading about the proper technique on the Internet
    B. viewing videos of his or her own performances
    C. viewing videos of other professional wrestlers
    D. buying technology related equipment to support physical activities

**Answer:** B

**Explanation:** Viewing self-performance is a way to see mistakes and locate areas of improvement.

**QUESTION 120**

Below are the spectrum styles in regards to the teaching style in physical education. Which of the following is incorrectly matched?

| Letter | Spectrum Style | Learning Intentions | Physical Education Example |
|--------|---------------|---------------------|----------------------------|
| A | Command | Physical: Motor skill sequisition | Performing a somersault on a trampoline |
| B | Practice | Physical: Motor skill development | Groups of four practice the "dig" in volleyball |
| C | Reciprocal | Social: Working with others. Cognitive observing, analysis | In twos, practice the set shot in basketball. |
| D | Self-check | Independent thinking and increase confidence | Shot putt in athletics. Success criteria on teaching card. |

**Answer:** D

**Explanation:** Self-check are learners assessing themselves in comparison to criteria sheets established by a teacher.

## QUESTION 121

Dodgeball does provide a means of practicing some important physical skills. Which of the following is not a skill obtained through dodgeball?

- A. running
- B. hiding
- C. catching
- D. throwing

**Answer:** B

**Explanation:** In dodgeball, individuals are trying to run away from the ball not to be hit, but there is no hiding being done. Dodgeball also requires catching the ball to throw at individuals.

## QUESTION 122

The following quote is from a paper: "Even if your child's school provides daily P.E. classes, parents should still make an effort to be active role models by enjoying 60 minutes of physical activity per day…it's a fact that active parents have active children, so to ensure children reap the benefits of physical activity, such as muscle strength, cardiovascular health, and flexibility, children need to be exposed to an active lifestyle at home."

The above quote highlights the importance of:

- A. how school and community impact the attitude of children for physical education
- B. how setting set times and days for periodic exercise can improve health
- C. how parents impact the motivation of children for physical education
- D. the importance of role a model to ensure the curriculum of physical education is improving

**Answer:** C

**Explanation:** The quote clearly is related to how parents impact the motivation of children for physical education.

## QUESTION 123

Of the following students, who is likely to lose weight safely?

| Letter | Name | Daily Intake (calories) | Daily Expenditure (calories) |
|--------|------|-------------------------|------------------------------|
| A | Ray | 4,000 | 4,000 |
| B | Jake | 4,000 | 3,000 |
| C | Tommy | 3,000 | 3,800 |
| D | Alex | 2,000 | 5,000 |

**Answer:** C

**Explanation:** Ray's intake and expenditure is the same, so losing weight might not be likely. Jake's intake is greater than expenditure, so he will not lose weight. Alex's intake is way lower than his expenditure, so he may lose weight, but not in a safe manner. Tommy's intake is 3,000 calories, and his expenditure is reasonably more. Tommy can lose weight safely.

## QUESTION 124

A physical education teacher can follow which of the following in the beginning of the school year to establish the best classroom management?

A. invite parents to the first day of class and go over the rules
B. post rules on the front door and around the classroom and complete introductions
C. establish rules and review them with students, create a record-keeping system, and teach students a signal to stop activity
D. have rules posted on walls, have open gym period, and create a record keeping system

**Answer:** C

**Explanation:** Rules are important in school and physical education classes along with record keeping. Knowing when to stop an activity is important in physical education classes.

**QUESTION 125**

At James Intermediate School, a second grade physical education instructor is planning an activity where she will have the students walk around the school track field. Time to time the teacher will inform the students to increase their speed until it becomes hard to communicate with their partner. In undertaking this approach, the teacher is most likely trying to increase student awareness in which of the following principles?

    A.  intensity
    B.  time
    C.  force
    D.  frequency

**Answer:** A

**Explanation:** The teacher is asking the students to do activity that is more intense by increasing speed to the point where it becomes difficult to communicate with their partner.

# ILTS Physical Education 144

## Illinois Licensure Testing System

Made in the USA
Monee, IL
14 December 2021